SIX POPES

A SON OF THE CHURCH REMEMBERS

MONSIGNOR
HILARY C. FRANCO
STD, JCL, MA (Soc)

with

ANTHONY FLOOD

Humanix Books
www.humanixbooks.com

Humanix Books

Six Popes
Copyright © 2021 by Humanix Books
All rights reserved

Humanix Books, P.O. Box 20989, West Palm Beach, FL 33416, USA
www.humanixbooks.com | info@humanixbooks.com

Humanix Books is a division of Humanix Publishing, LLC. Its
trademark, consisting of the word "Humanix," is registered in the
Patent and Trademark Office and in other countries.

For photography credit information, please visit
www.humanixbooks.com/SixPopes or write to
info@humanixbooks.com.

ISBN: 978-163006-133-3 (Hardcover)
ISBN: 978-163006-134-0 (E-book)

Printed in the United States of America
10 9 8 7 6 5 4 3 2 1

Memoria minuitur nisi eam exerceas.

[Memory diminishes if you do not exercise it.]

CICERO

Contents

                  to Turtle Bay................... 141

Chapter Twelve   The Church of Benedict, Francis,
                  and the Future................. 159

                  Acknowledgments.............. 169

                  Index....................... 171

Introduction

Historia, magistra vitae.
[History, the teacher of life.]

CICERO

When, over 65 years ago, God called me to be a priest and I said "Yes!" I set off on a journey that would involve *both* leading people to Heaven *and* saving them from Hell.* Along the way I accumulated a treasure trove of memories.

Even though born during the reign of Pope Pius XI (r. 1922–1939), his successor, Pius XII (r. 1939–1958), was the first pope of whom I was cognizant. There were, however, six men who became popes whom, as seminarian and priest, I came to know personally. They are points of departure for the story of this son of the Church.

It's the story of a kid who, by the grace of God, rose from the streets of Belmont—an Italian-American neighborhood in the Bronx that helped create doo-wop music—to serve Christ's Church and spread His message of divine love. I saw the human race's great possibilities alongside its tragically missed opportunities—the mansions of the super-rich not far

---

* Dag Hammarskjöld once said the United Nations "was not created in order to bring us to heaven, but in order to save us from hell." "Address by Secretary-General Dag Hammarskjöld at University of California Convocation, Berkeley, California," May 13, 1954.

from the hovels of the abysmally poor. I saw the latter's champions in the saints whom it was my privilege to know.

For many years, friends and family have encouraged me to "write a book." Neither they (nor I, for that matter) saw me as a writer. Yes, I've served the Church as a priest under six popes, but I do not claim to have been an intimate of all of them.

But I do claim to be a witness. I have been a witness to the lives of good and great Roman Catholics, and in this book I'll share choice recollections from my time with Archbishop Fulton Sheen and working in the Vatican for Saint John Paul II, among other Fishermen.

My life's outline, trajectory, and contents are gifts from God, Who, in His infinite mercy and through His Blessed Mother's intercession, bestowed this grace on me. I did nothing to merit it. An extra grace has been my continued ability—aided by diaries kept faithfully since my ordination—to recall dates and events accurately at my not-so-young age and set them before you.

This is inexplicable to me apart from the Almighty's quiet but persistent work through me. As it turns out, my witness in this book may help complete my mission to the Church and Our Lord. I am reminded of Paul's instruction to Philemon: "I pray that the sharing of your faith may become effective for the full knowledge of every good thing that is in us for the sake of Christ" (Philemon 1:6). I hope the fruit of this effort convinces you that a life of service to God in Jesus Christ, fortified by His Blessed Mother's intercession, can make a difference in this sin-ravaged world.

Even if it begins in the *quartiere* of Belmont.

Ad Jesum per Mariam.

ONE

Bronx Kid

Life is like a cash register, in that every account,
every thought, every deed, like every sale,
is registered and recorded.

FULTON J. SHEEN

The last day of non–Leap Year in February is the 28th. In 2013, it was last in a historically significant way: it was the last day Joseph Ratzinger served the Catholic Church as Pope Benedict XVI. For on that day he took the unprecedented step of resigning his papacy. Not two weeks later, on March 13th, a conclave chose his successor, Jorge Mario Bergoglio, who, as an Argentinian and Jesuit, also made history. Not in over 500 years have two popes been contemporaries.

That spring, I reached the milestone age of 80. I was serving as pastor of Saint Augustine's in Ossining, New York, about which more in due course. My "retirement" was around the corner, but still a season away. A papal transition after a papal retirement moved thoughts of my own possible transition to my mind's back burner.

I was born in a historic era. (So are we all, but some are more historic than others.) As the administrations of President Franklin D. Roosevelt, New York Mayor Fiorello La Guardia, and Pope Pius XI overlapped each other, I entered the world on July 16, 1932. For this kid, there was one president, one mayor, one pope.

My neighborhood was Belmont, near 187th Street and Crotona and Arthur Avenues in the Bronx. This locale was home to one of the leading doo-wop groups, the Belmonts; two of them grew up on Belmont Avenue.

The Italian immigrants who dominated Belmont made for great lore, the stuff of movies like Scorsese's *GoodFellas* and *Raging Bull*. Hollywood myths aside, however, Belmont was populated by hardworking Italian-Americans who loved their families, their country, and their Church.

We shopped in the Arthur Avenue Market when it was new, one of many vendor consolidations created by Mayor La Guardia in the thirties and forties to replace the myriads of street-clogging pushcarts and liberate the pedestrian sidewalks.

The first wave of Italian immigration hit America's shores in the 1880s; the second, around the turn of the twentieth century, booming after World War I. Many of the immigrants, settling in Belmont, gave Arthur Avenue the Italian identity it has to this day. Among them were my parents.

My mother, Maria Catalina Scali, a primary school teacher for 41 years, was always after us—especially me!—to get an education. An immigrant from Italy's Calabria region, she loved her Italian culture and didn't let us speak English at home. We had to speak "real" Italian, not a dialect. Anyone who speaks with me can hear its echoes in my voice.

My father, Tommaso ("Thomas" as in his 1927 American passport) Franco, also a native Calabrese, arrived in America as a young man. Coming from a well-to-do family, he had been under no economic pressure to emigrate. He did, however, imbibe socialist ideas from the old country. An old-school socialist, but no communist, he wanted to help new immigrants "make it" in their adopted homeland. Before settling in the Bronx, his goal was to start a newspaper in Clarksburg, West Virginia, whose coal mining jobs had attracted so many of them.

He did not find immigrant life easy, coming as he did from a well-groomed Catholic family which, in the course of a century, had given the Church at least three priests: my great-uncle Don Ilario Franco, a well-known nineteenth-century professor of classics; his brother, Archpriest Tommaso Franco; and my uncle Father Ilario Franco, who had come to America to serve Italian immigrants and was incardinated in the Archdiocese of New York.

One Sunday an Irish priest barred my father's entrance to a church where he had intended to go for Mass. He was told to go to church in the basement. A handsome and powerful young man, Dad didn't take disrespect kindly. "I had a choice," he told me many years later. "Push the priest aside (which would have only angered his people) or leave. I left." He never attempted to set foot in a church again until the day of my ordination.

Dad was all about taking care of people, a trait I wanted to emulate. As a teenager I shared with him inklings of my vocation, but he wasn't thrilled. At my ordination, however, he presented me with a parchment on which his own "ten commandments" were inscribed. The first? "Take care of the people." That directive has never been far from my thoughts since that day during the past six-and-a-half decades. And so, my goal as a priest was always to be with the people of God. Not serve them at a distance (although sometimes I had no choice), but to be *with* them. I attribute this attitude to Dad's social-minded, if not socialist, sensibilities and their influence on me.

As a youngster I aspired to be, not a policeman, fireman, or soldier, but an actor. My mother encouraged my proclivity to declaim at the drop of a hat, which I did with any poetry I memorized. When directing the liturgy, the priest is center-stage on the altar—facing the tabernacle in the traditional Mass—reenacting the drama of the Sacrifice on Calvary. That suited me to a T.

With Dad having "unchurched" himself, Mom assumed responsibility for her children's religious education. As a boy, I accepted the Catholic faith more or less passively. I thought no more about it than my chums did. But one day the sight of an elderly priest in the Manhattan neighborhood where I was working provoked me to ask: "What plans does the good Lord have for me?" I was barely 18; no vocation had entered my mind until that time.

Upon my return to America from Rome as a priest—much more on that later—I was assigned for three months to Our Lady of Mount Carmel, a Bronx church. Then Saint Dominic's on Unionport Road, also in the Bronx, was home for me for almost two years (while I earned a master's in sociology at Fordham University). I was then transferred to Assumption Parish in New Brighton, Staten Island, a borough of New York, at that time connected to the rest of city only by ferry. (The Verrazzano Bridge, which connects Staten Island to Brooklyn, opened in 1964.) I served at Assumption in Staten Island for three years. As there was no shortage of pastoral outlets for my energy, I enjoyed every day of these assignments. My wish to be *with* the people was fulfilled in abundance.

But God had other plans for me.

When the fifties began and before I voyaged to Rome, I was but one of Fulton J. Sheen's millions of fans. An American Catholic bishop, Sheen was a renowned philosopher, prolific writer, and television star whose ratings rivaled those of Milton Berle ("Mr. Television") and Frank Sinatra ("The Voice"). An admirer of Sheen's based on what I had read—pretty much every word he'd ever published—I eagerly looked forward to his TV show *Life Is Worth Living*, which aired on the DuMont network on Tuesday nights at 8:00 p.m. With as many as 10 million viewers hanging on his every word, the show's success rivaled that of Berle's *Texaco Star Theater*.

As a Roman university student in 1954, the year Pope Pius X was canonized, I caught a view of Sheen at a distance. During the canonization ceremony, in which the saintly pope's casketed body was carried, Sheen struck a handsome, statuesque figure. His head of neatly combed black hair was revealed only at the Mass's consecration, when prelates had their mitres removed.

I could not then imagine that by the decade's close, Sheen would promote me from fan to friend to trusted assistant and confidant. As the last surviving member of his household, I have had the privilege of receiving over 100 handwritten letters from him, the final one coming a little over a month before he died in 1979.

My earlier book, *Bishop Fulton J. Sheen: Mentor and Friend*, tells that story, some episodes of which I'll retrace while adding a few details. As both a witness to his saintliness and a friend, I've been devoted to the cause of Sheen's beatification, which proceeds at a snail's pace as I write. It's usually a slow process, and Sheen's is no exception. There have been ups and downs. Here are a few.

Sheen's beatification had been set for December 21, 2019, but the Diocese of Rochester, New York, where he had served as bishop for three years in the late sixties, wants to examine how he handled clerical abuse accusations against priests under his authority. The Vatican has suspended the cause indefinitely.

In the meanwhile, a scandalous tug-of-war over Sheen's mortal remains transpired between Catholic dioceses. On many occasions he made it clear to me that he wished to be buried in New York. Yes, Peoria, Illinois, was his hometown and city of his priestly ordination, but there's no evidence he wanted to be buried there. All the evidence we have goes the other way.

The rope-pulling contest began when Mrs. Joan Cunningham, a niece of Bishop Sheen's who had been unhappy with the interment of her uncle's remains under Saint Patrick's Cathedral's main altar, requested they be translated to Peoria. Justice Arlene Bluth of the Supreme Court's New York County Petition Court granted this on November 17, 2016. On February 6, 2018, the Appellate Division of the New York State Supreme Court reversed Justice Bluth's decision. The court ruled that disinterment couldn't occur until an evidentiary hearing was held. The original decision to translate Sheen's remains to Peoria was reinstated. On June 9, 2019, the Archdiocese of New York gave up the effort to keep Sheen's remains. They traveled a few weeks later to Saint Mary's Cathedral in Peoria.

To say I'm disappointed by this outcome is to understate things. As I recorded at the time:

> ...the appellate justices recognized that in Justice Bluth's 2016 decision, she "failed to give appropriate consideration to the affidavit of Monsignor Franco and too narrowly defined the inquiry into Archbishop Sheen's wishes." It added, "Monsignor Franco stated that Archbishop Sheen had repeatedly expressed his 'desire to remain in New York even after his death.' Contrary to the motion court's conclusion, a fair reading of this alleged exchange, if it is true, is that Archbishop Sheen wished his body to remain somewhere in New York.... The petition court ... improperly deferred to the family's wishes, merely because Archbishop Sheen's remains did not end up in Calvary Cemetery [where he had bought a plot for his burial], and without a full exploration of Archbishop Sheen's desires."

Unambiguously, Sheen wished to be buried in New York. But this wish was not to be granted. May ours for his beatification receive a favorable answer. In my lifetime, God willing!

TWO

My Roman Formation

Vivo ego, iam non ego.
Vivit vero in me Christus!

[It is not I who lives.
It is Christ who lives in me!]

GALATIANS: 2:20

In 1939, when I turned seven, I was blissfully unaware of the world beyond Belmont. Dictatorships sprang up in Europe and Asia, and the winds of the Second World War blew with gale force as Germany invaded Poland. Great churchmen who would affect my life were either behind the scenes or already on the world stage.

On March 2nd of the year, Cardinal Eugenio Pacelli, then the Vatican's Secretary of State, ascended to Peter's throne. To honor his predecessor Pius XI, who had died a few weeks before, Pacelli took his name, becoming Pius XII. A Roman aristocrat, Pacelli was raised to the Church's diplomatic corps, but for all his training and strenuous work as Secretary of State, he couldn't prevent the Church—the world-immersed Body of Christ—from being drawn into the maelstrom of World War II.

Pastor Angelicus, a film Pius XII commissioned in 1942, captured his desire to remain connected to God's people even as war raged around them. His presence in Rome during the bombardments of the neighborhood of San Lorenzo fuori le

Mura encouraged and inspired Rome's citizens. After the war, however, he was on the receiving end of the unfounded slander that the Vatican's posture toward Hitler's regime—*his* posture—was that of leniency, that he was, at best, indifferent to the Holocaust.

For Catholics and non-Catholics alike, including Alcide De Gasperi and other future leaders, the Holy Father during the war turned the Vatican and the extraterritorial places connected to this city-state (where the Nazis could not enter) into safe houses. In a 1951 address to a joint session of Congress while the United States was helping to reconstruct Europe, De Gasperi exemplified the Italian people's indomitable will to rebuild their country. I remember the disheveled coat this Italian Prime Minister and founder of the Christian Democratic Party wore to this occasion, a reminder of the state of Italy's economy even six years after the war's end. Although the calumny of his being indifferent to genocide inflicted suffering upon him, Pius XII rose above it and achieved great things for the Church and humanity.

I would like to mention here that a wonderful New Yorker of the Jewish Faith, my friend Gary Krupp, founded The Pave the Way Foundation, whose aim is to gather documentation on the actions of Pius XII in favor of the Jews during the war. The Foundation has already done a tremendous job in this, and Mr. Krupp and his wife Meredith have received a Papal Honor for the work in the Foundation.

I was a boy when Pius XI was pope, but the first pope to enter my consciousness was Pius XII. In 1950, eight years after *Pastor Angelicus*, I answered the call to the priesthood at the age of 18. The Holy Father had proclaimed it a Holy Year, the first postwar Jubilee Year. The faithful flocked to Rome as never before. Still a teenager, but in spirit already Romeward bound, I eagerly absorbed all the coverage I could find. The sight of pilgrims entering Saint Peter's Basilica through the Holy Doors, the solemnity and pageantry of the ceremonies there and elsewhere in the Eternal City, impressed me deeply.

My mind now made up, any interest I once may have had in becoming something other than a priest evaporated. In those days, young people weren't distracted by so many options as they now seem to be. Once we decided upon a course of action, we focused on it. As Paul wrote, "When I was a child . . . I thought as a child." A cornucopia of choices is a childish thing, something a young man needs to put away (1 Corinthians 13:11), which I did.

My priestly formation at the Pontifical Lateran University and the Pontifical Roman Seminary (PRS), then the number one seminary in the world, was rigorous. I was sent there rather than to the North American College (NAC) because the latter was still being renovated after the war. For that rebuilding initiative we owe a lot to the New York archbishop, Francis Cardinal Spellman.

On my PRS campus, the buildings had radiators, but they were apparently unused—and unheated! One reason (or excuse) we were given was that, were we to traverse the courtyard from one heated building to another, we might catch a cold.

After dinner there was recreation, which might keep our bodies moving and warm. "Dinner," what we Yanks called lunch, was around one, the day's main meal for Italians. On my first day of such recreation, I went upstairs to my room to change. (Our rooms were small, but private, a luxury in those days.) After donning my sport briefs I returned to the *cortile* (recreation courtyard) where a soccer ball awaited me. That was it—no other sports! My fellow seminarians, still cassocked, were shocked to see me in this apparel. The "prefect," Sergio Goretti (a future Bishop of Assisi), approached me.

"What are you doing? This is a scandal!"

"Well, you said there'd be recreation, so I dressed for kicking around a soccer ball."

"All right . . . Come with me."

Up to my room we went.

"Put on your cassock."

"How can I see the ball with *that* on?!"

"Put it on! Take off your belt and put it over the cassock. Now, pull your cassock, and you'll see the ball in front of you."

After an hour of running in a thick cassock, I was a perspiring mess; our rooms had no showers. Heading to the communal showers, I couldn't evade my prefect's gaze.

"Where are you going?!"

"To take a shower . . . ?"

"Showers are once a week. No showers now!"

"But I'm sweaty now! What am I going to do?"

"Use the faucets we're lucky to have in our rooms."

Faucets that delivered cold water.

Our formation was strict, but I now see how it fortified me for the challenges ahead. It instilled habits that would stand us in good stead for the rest of our lives. For that I'll always be grateful.

The NAC didn't have the amenities of the Roman Seminary, including, as I mentioned, private rooms. Penetrating their thick doors, however, was the bell that roused us from our slumber. Filling the corridors by 6:30 a.m. and outfitted in cassocks *sans* collars, but not yet washed, we knelt outside those doors. One man would lead us in praying three Hail Marys (which I still do daily, but my knees no longer permit kneeling).

The meals were unforgettable. There were no better chefs than those nuns from northern Italy. I ate everything! At our first breakfast, a classmate wanted more coffee, but didn't know how to ask for it in Italian. (He was from Philadelphia.) Thanks to Mom's expert tutelage, my Italian was perfect, and thus the first step in my career as a translator. A decade or so later, I'd use this skill for real-time translations for American bishops during the Second Vatican Council.

Travel to and from the United States wasn't cheap, so going home for summer vacation was out of the question. Like other Roman seminaries, however, ours had a summer place not far from the Eternal City, beautiful Roccantica in the Rieti province. That's where I summered. Years before, the seminary used to have a villa in the Dolomites, splendid for mountain lovers, I suppose, but we found Roccantica perfect. It was situated in the mountains, but not so remote that we couldn't get pastoral experience in nearby parishes. Invariably we'd welcome eminent alumni who'd come to visit, like Monsignor (later on Cardinal) Domenico Tardini or the newly created cardinal, Alfredo Ottaviani, and so many others.

Holy Week and Easter were painstakingly prepared. The Roman Seminary was part of the Pontifical (Papal) Family. If

Saint Peter's Basilica held a major event, we were expected to participate. A solemn occasion (for example, a canonization) could last four hours. To prepare to go outdoors, we donned cassocks, violet like those worn by monsignors in Pius X's day, outfitted with a red sash and buttons, floppy black hats, and a violet wool cloak, or *soprana*. We looked like monsignors even then. But you can only imagine what being wrapped in that material was like under the Roman sun!

Public transportation was off-limits. We rose early, attended chapel, and spent half an hour of preached meditation before heading off to Saint Peter's. Near the end of my time there, they'd let us go in pairs. We'd head back after a four- or five-hour ceremony. A real workout! Some afternoons we'd enjoy a *passegiata*, or stroll. Two or three times a week—always together and properly attired—we were allowed to walk from, say, the Archbasilica of Saint John Lateran to the Basilica of Saint Mary Major or to another church to visit the Blessed Sacrament. That consumed another hour, hour-and-a-half. Classes, study, and prayer occupied us until lights-out.

In my mind's eye I still see Pius XII during the solemn ceremonies being conveyed from the rear of the Basilica of Saint Peter on his ceremonial chair, the *sedia gestatoria*, as trumpets sounded "Charles Gounod's Pontifical Anthem." How could I not be overwhelmed?

Yet I found something about the ceremony spiritually "off." Those scarlet trains and luxurious capes didn't sit well with me. The fine material that trailed behind the pontiffs seemed to rival corridors in length, symptoms of spiritual tone-deafness. I still feel that way. Not until Pope Paul VI was the amount of such regalia greatly reduced.

When I was about 20, a seminary alumnus and its former spiritual director was named archbishop. Scheduled to visit Padre Pio da Pietrelcina, His Excellency invited me to join him in attending one of Padre Pio's masses in his convent church in a small town near Bari. This unexpected invitation inaugurated another blessing in my life.

Every morning at 6:30, Padre Pio said Mass in the small church of Santa Maria delle Grazie in San Giovanni Rotondo, attached to the convent of the Capuchin Fathers. To attend that Mass, people began lining up outside the church long before its doors swung open. Maybe because I was the only seminarian that morning, or maybe because I was accompanying the archbishop (well known to the Franciscans there), I was asked to serve at Padre Pio's Mass—which finished around 9:30! During the Mass, Padre Pio would go into ecstasy, a spiritual state in which one transcends ordinary experience. It was clear to me that for Padre Pio, "ecstasy" literally, not figuratively, described his experience. None of us felt that three hours had passed.

At the end of Mass, Padre Pio, who had received Christ's stigmata in 1910, turned to me:

"*Giovanotto* [Young man], *these wonderful people want to touch my hands, but I don't feel well this morning. Please . . . would you take me to my cell through the sacristy?*"

I helped him remove his vestments in the sacristy, a delicate task due to the stigmata, the open wounds that his hands bore. Upon then accompanying Padre Pio to his cell, I had the privilege of a private chat and a blessing. Today, he's Saint Padre Pio.

We never met again after that. When he died on September 23, 1968, I had been working in Rome for three months within the new Prefecture for Economic Affairs of the Holy See. (More on that later.) The Vatican ensured the continuance of Padre Pio's work, embodied in Casa Sollievo della Sofferenza (Home for the Relief of the Suffering), the hospital he had founded in San Giovanni Rotondo.

I cannot say I foresaw this manifestly holy man's canonization, but neither can I say it surprised me. I was present at the solemn ceremony of his canonization in Saint Peter's Square on June 16, 2002.

ᴄᴏᴑᴑᴑ

Christmas season in Rome is always inspirational, and my first was no exception. Preparing for Advent meant learning to sing Gregorian chants. After Midnight Mass at Christmas, around 1:30 a.m., we were served a kind of punch, a revered seminary tradition.

By today's standards, seminarians were cut off from the outside world. Calling home was expensive; at our disposal there was, maybe, one phone in the complex; I think the seminary's rector had one. I loved my natural family, but now I had a new family, a spiritual one. My folks knew that as a priest, I devoted myself to God and His people. My brother, Emilio, who had studied medicine, could take care of himself. My family's finances were in good shape. I couldn't risk letting the hustle and bustle of life in the United States take my priestly formation off course.

But we could write letters. Mom, who lived to be 98, kept mine. They weren't long, but they captured my affection for Mom, Dad, Emilio, and everybody else. I shared my seminary experiences, trying to convey to them the grandeur of the Eternal City. I literally penned these letters: a typewriter didn't come into my possession until I began to prepare my dissertation. (When I bought my Olympia in 1956, I felt I was the luckiest man in the world.) I doubt my letters have survived; I'd love to be proven wrong.

A grounding in philosophy prepared me for the theological studies that gave rein to my interest in biblical theology and Hebrew, the language of most of the Old Testament. It was love at first sight. For one who was brought up with only the Roman alphabet, deciphering Hebrew script was a kind of play.

I tried to dig beneath the text's surface. The creation narratives in Genesis mesmerized me. One day I was studying the book of Genesis. "Wait a minute," I thought. "We're always talking about the *earthly* paradise. But what does this mean?" I could prove from the text that there was no such thing. For one thing, there are different Hebrew words for "earth" and "garden." One little word, the Hebrew preposition *min*, "from," provoked an unconventional thought in my mind: the four rivers of Genesis 2:10-14 flowed from the garden, the story's larger context, but we're told Adam and Eve were thrown out of the garden *onto* the earth (*adamah*)!

I now had my doctoral thesis. After jotting down the essentials of my bright idea, I took my notes to Monsignor Ermenegildo Florit, the learned professor of Scripture at the Lateran University. His initial reaction was:

"No, no, no!"

It took a day for my argument to sink in.

"Young man, I went through the text. You're right. But let's not pursue this."

He was promoted soon afterward, eventually becoming Cardinal Archbishop of Florence. That meant he had to hand off his teaching duties to someone else. Our new professor was Monsignor Salvatore Garofalo, a widely published biblical scholar. I eagerly put my interpretation before him.

"How about this?"

With an encouraging smile, he conceded:

"Young man, you do have a point. . . . You should pursue this!"

Pursue it I did, finishing with one of the highest grades at the university.

I defended my dissertation on July 3, 1956, receiving the highest possible grade. I continued to conduct research at the Biblical Institute auditing the classes of, and getting advice from, Alberto Vaccari, SJ (1875–1965), a scholar at the Pontifical Biblical Institute (*Biblicum*).

As a member of the American Biblical Association, I've tried to keep up my interest in biblical studies. Eventually I was invited to write entries for *The New Catholic Encyclopedia*, including one on "Slavery in the Old Testament," which was accepted.

Another lifelong interest has been sociology, one more fruit of my pastoral orientation and my father's toward social action. My mentor was Father Joseph Fitzpatrick, Dean of Sociology at Fordham University, a pioneer in the field. He was also an exemplary priest, one whom I wanted to emulate. (More about him later.)

Economic theories, when implemented by government, affect the lives of the people I interact with as a priest. Economics looms large in their lives. I plunged into its study and use what I learned to this day. For me, economics is not only about helping someone get a job. It's also about understanding, say, how unemployment can descend upon people like a natural disaster, something beyond human control. But having sound economic policy is *not* beyond human control.

Essential to my grasp of these matters has been the Church's social teaching, starting with Leo XIII's *Rerum Novarum* (1891) and arriving at Saint John XXIII's *Pacem in Terris* (1963), Paul VI's *Populorum Progressio* (1967), and Pope Francis's *Laudato Si'* (2015). In my opinion, we find in these encyclicals and in *Gaudium et Spes*—the Second Vatican Council's *Pastoral Constitution on the Church in the Modern World*—the principles that can corner our world's economic problems.

THREE

Angelo Roncalli: Fellow Alumnus, Pope, and Saint

A peaceful man does more good than a learned one.

POPE JOHN XXIII

 e✺✺✺∞

A ngelo Giuseppe Roncalli, now known to history as
Saint John XXIII, was an alumnus of the world's premier Catholic seminary, the Pontifical Roman Seminary. My
seminary.

Alumni would often visit. Some were nuncios (ambassa-
dors of the Holy See), some cardinals, others parish priests.
They freely shared their memories and experiences with us.
One visitor during my time there was Roncalli, later Patriarch
of Venice and Cardinal Priest of Santa Prisca. He was jolly and
rotund, but no longer young. He was an archbishop and nuncio to Paris. One day after a big lunch we stood around him in
the courtyard, preferring his stories to any recreation. Roncalli
impressed me as a person. There was no hint of what the near
future held for him.

Here's how he became nuncio in Paris. The Allies had lib-
erated the City of Lights on August 25, 1944; the next day,
General Charles de Gaulle returned from exile (in Great
Britain) to become the first Chairman of the Provisional
Government of the French Republic. As the year drew to a

close, tradition would have the Dean of the Diplomatic Corps deliver the New Year's greeting. In Catholic countries the dean is the apostolic nuncio. That position was held by Archbishop (later Cardinal) Valerio Valeri, as he had since 1936.

Unfortunately, Valeri had also worked closely with France's Vichy government, which collaborated with France's German occupiers. The last thing de Gaulle wanted was a man connected with that recent past greeting him on New Year's Eve. Through diplomatic channels de Gaulle voiced his desire for a new nuncio.

Pope Pius XII had intended to appoint Archbishop Giuseppe Fietta, then Argentina's nuncio, but his heart medically ruled out his flying to Europe. No ship could get him to Paris by January 1, 1945.

Pius met de Gaulle's request for a new nuncio to Paris by naming the well-liked Angelo Roncalli. What I learned later at the Apostolic Delegation in Washington was that Pius did this over the objections of then–Pro-Secretary of State Domenico Tardini. Monsignor (later Cardinal) Francesco Colasuonno told me Tardini took a dim view of Roncalli's promotion. (Tardini was a seminarian at the Pontifical Roman Seminary around the same time as Roncalli, and there was apparently some "history" between the two men.) Pius XII heard Tardini out, but directed him:

"Call Roncalli."

"Your Holiness, Roncalli, of all people! He can create problems!"

The pope smiled.

"No, call Roncalli."

Roncalli told us seminarians, "I arrived in Rome, and went straight to Tardini, my immediate superior."

"I had nothing to do with this!" Tardini told Roncalli. *"You'd better see the pope!"*

Roncalli opened with:

"It's probably a case of omonimia *(homonymy), and one mis-hears one name as another. Perhaps Your Holiness had somebody else in mind."*

"No, I want you to go to Paris."

Roncalli was named nuncio two days before Christmas, 1944. Had he been unable to get to Paris in time for New Year's, the ceremonial duty would have fallen to the most senior member of France's diplomatic corps—Aleksandr Bogomolov, the Russian ambassador. De Gaulle no less cordially objected to having a Russian addressing him as his presidential term commenced. (As though foreseeing Stalin's expansionist aims, de Gaulle was wary of his foreign agents.)

The day arrived. As Bogomolov was preparing to give his New Year's address, Roncalli entered a magnificent room filled with members of the diplomatic corps. The Russian ambassador was not amused. Knowing French as well as he did, Roncalli gave a beautiful talk.

"Now," he told us, "I had a problem with the Russian ambassador and wasn't sure how to handle it. At one of our usual diplomatic receptions, I approached him and said, 'Your Excellency, I don't know how to say this . . . We may not have much in common, but there's one thing we *do* have in common: our belly.' I gently poked his, which was as prominent as mine. He laughed, and we became the greatest of friends."

The presidents of France, Spain, and Portugal had the privilege of placing the cardinalatial *biretta*, the cardinal's red hat, on newly created cardinals. So when Roncalli left Paris in 1953 to become Patriarch of Venice and Cardinal-Priest of Santa Prisca, he received his *biretta* not from the pope, but from Vincent Auriol, France's president. Auriol was not Catholic, but he respected and admired the nuncio. Sad to see Roncalli go, Bogomolov, his friend for almost nine years, accompanied him to the airport for an emotional *au revoir!*

Roncalli had a devotion to *La Madonna della Fiducia*, Our Lady of Confidence, the Madonna of the Roman Seminary. Whenever in Rome, he'd always visit Her, a habit he maintained as pope. During one of our after-dinner chats, he told us about France's worker-priest movement. Some priests wanted to be *both* priests *and* members of the working class. This posed a challenge to ecclesiastical authority, and as nuncio, Roncalli had to meet it. One day Roncalli's secretary told him:

"Maurice Thorez, the Secretary of the Communist Party of France, wants you to receive him to discuss the worker-priests issue."

Roncalli agreed to receive Thorez. "But I gave him an audience of only twenty minutes."

Thorez and his secretary were ushered in. Roncalli held forth with his guests for exactly 20 minutes ... on the wines of Northern Italy! Then:

"So sorry: I have another appointment."

Thorez turned to his secretary:

"At last, someone shrewder than me!"

As the dean of Paris's diplomatic corps, Roncalli was regularly invited to receptions and dinners. At one of them an ambassador's wife wore a dress that, shall we say, didn't leave enough to the imagination. *Décolleté* as the French say.

"When the fruit was served, I offered her an apple."

"Oh, thank you so much!"

"'You know,' I told her, 'there's a beautiful story in the Bible about a lady who took an apple and then realized she wasn't fully dressed.'

"She'd always be covered up whenever I saw her after that!"

As I mentioned, Angelo Giuseppe Roncalli was created cardinal during the 1953 consistory. The cardinals form the pope's senate, as it were, but they are also Rome's bishops (they are seven cardinal bishops for the so called suburbicarian dioceses) and presbyters, who bear titles that relate them to particular churches in the Eternal City and surrounding territories. Roncalli's titular church was Santa Prisca on the Aventine Hill. We seminarians were called to serve at his installation, and our choir chanted for our prestigious alumnus.

From the choir loft, I had a bird's-eye view of the ceremony. Cardinals then wore ermine robes over which fell a cape, which had an opening for the head. There we were, ready to chant, but the moment Roncalli was to receive the cape, Monsignor Aluffi, the pontifical master of ceremonies, couldn't find the opening! His patience gone, Roncalli grabbed the cape from the hapless Aluffi and quickly found the elusive hole. We suppressed guffaws.

No one, least of all Roncalli, could imagine his election to the papacy. Before leaving Rome for the conclave that would elect Pius XII's successor, Venice's portly patriarch was fitted for his own casket—done routinely for prelates well in advance of their earthly demise. Everyone assumed he'd return from the conclave to Venice and die there. God had other plans.

Angelo Giuseppe Roncalli was elected pope on the 28th of October 1958. I'd see him again at the Second Vatican Council, but there were also preconciliar meetings where we'd be granted an audience. During a course of studies in Ariccia, a town on Rome's outskirts, we had our picture taken with him as pope, a picture I still treasure. In my mind's eye he's never perched on a throne, but always a friend mingling among us.

FOUR

Back Home: Cheating Death, and My Southern Adventure

The spirit of humility is sweeter than honey,
and those who nourish themselves
with this honey produce sweet fruit.

SAINT ANTHONY OF PADUA

The years of university training and priestly formation were now in my rearview mirror. I was 22, but you had to be at least 24 to be ordained a priest in those days (according to canon law). You could ask for a special dispensation from an office in the Vatican Curia, but only the pope could grant one for a 22-year-old.

And grant it he did. I would have waited two more years if I had to, but with a papal decree in hand, I didn't.

I was ordained on April 9, 1955. Some who knew me may have thought, "Father Hilary is heading toward an academic or a diplomatic career," but "career" never entered my mind. Would my academic pursuits keep me from the people? I hoped not.

My studies took four years plus another year to research and write my doctoral dissertation, which I defended, as noted earlier, on July 3, 1956. My uncle, Father Ilario Franco, then pastor of the (now-closed) Yonkers parish of Saint Anthony's, wired funds to book my passage on the *SS Andrea Doria*. I was scheduled to depart July 17th. Uncle Ilario called:

"Why wait two weeks? Can't you reserve a spot on a ship that leaves sooner?"

I called Società Italia to see if there was an earlier U.S.-bound passage. The response:

"This is summer! Everybody's traveling. There's no chance of getting a ticket on another ship. The Andrea Doria *has a sister-ship, the* SS Cristoforo Colombo, *departing Naples on the ninth. Don't even think about it; every spot's taken."*

In 1956, flights were not as numerous, inexpensive, or frequent as they are today.

Early in the morning of July 7th, I got a call from the agency:

"A spot just opened up on the Cristoforo Colombo, *leaving on the ninth. If you want it, get to Naples!"*

Which I did.

I got seasick on that eight-days' voyage (my first, and so far, only!); after the Straits of Gibraltar, I lay in my cabin and remained horizontal for the rest of the trip. Arriving in New York on July 17th (my birthday!), I went to help my uncle at Saint Anthony's in Yonkers. Ten days later, on Saints Anne and Joachim's feast day, I was preparing to leave the rectory to celebrate Mass. Upon my reaching the main floor from my room, Amelia, our Italian housekeeper, approached me:

"Father, did you see what happened to the Andrea Doria?*"*

"No . . . ?"

"It collided with another ship . . ."

"Poor other ship," I blurted. No way anything could have happened to the unsinkable *Andrea Doria*.

When I returned for breakfast after Mass, Amelia reported:

"Father, it's the Andrea Doria *that's sinking."*

I rifled through my papers to find the number of the cabin I would have occupied and then scanned the passenger list in the *New York Times*. My eyes landed on the number: the man who took my place reported for the very paper I was reading. His compartment was among the first hit. He was among the dead. After passing through Gibraltar, I would have rested in my cabin, so that's where I'd most likely have been upon impact. I sat down to breakfast, stunned and mute.

Back from Rome in 1956, I got my first assignment. It was to Our Lady of Mount Carmel (OLMC) on Belmont Avenue and East 187th Street in the Bronx—my old neighborhood. The pastor, Auxiliary Bishop Joseph M. Pernicone, had been the first Italian-American bishop to be consecrated back in 1954 and my Uncle Ilario, OLMC's choir director and assistant priest, composed the Mass for the occasion. Everybody knew *that* Father Ilario Franco, but now there was another. To minimize confusion, I began to go by "Hilary," English for "Ilario." (Adding "Junior" was not an option.)

To say OLMC was a big parish would be an understatement. I'll never forget the day we had two dozen baptisms! We got many sick calls during the week and ministered to patients at nearby Fordham University's hospital. In the forties and fifties, OLMC's heyday, it was the largest Italian national parish in the United States. There were around 40,000 registered parishioners; and at least another 10,000 to 12,000 folks, overwhelmingly Italian, joined them in the pews. People came from all over to enjoy the atmosphere and traditions. Bishop Pernicone and his eight assistant priests (including this "kid") celebrated 16 Masses on Sunday alone. We said them not only in the main church, but also in the elementary school auditorium, Caffuzzi Hall. Every pew was filled. But nowadays, the parish is blessed to have a single priest.

OLMC served a small mission church on Arthur Avenue, dedicated to Saint Anthony. A Franciscan had staffed it for years before leaving the priesthood to get married, creating a scandal. We had to certify and validate every sacrament he had performed. The pastor, Bishop Pernicone, a canon lawyer, brought wisdom and skill to this process. He put an assistant priest, Father John Villani, in charge of Saint Anthony's. Father was active in OLMC's main rectory in addition to taking care of Saint Anthony's. When he went on vacation, I filled in.

❧◉❧

One sweltering summer day, instead of walking—as usual—to the main rectory for meals, I tried to make something to eat in the kitchen. No culinary expert, I assumed making a *frittata* (omelet) would be a no-brainer. I beat the eggs. My formidable intelligence grasped that since beaten eggs are liquid, they can be poured into a frying pan. I lit the stove.

"Perfect!," I emoted as the pan's contents solidified. I remember how my mother would jiggle the pan to facilitate the omelet's exit. But as I tried to mimic Mom's jiggle and slide, the omelet resisted. Too late did I realize I hadn't oiled the pan's surface! (No nonstick pans in those days.) Frustrated,

I stored the pan in the fridge and ran off to Fordham, knowing I'd be late for class.

Next morning, there was *no frittata in the fridge!* Joe, an elderly gent who helped around the sacristy, explained the absence:

"Oh, Father, was that ever so good!"

Thus the beginning and end of my cooking career. Now I settle for pushing a button on my Nespresso machine for a cup of coffee.

Saint Anthony's was a small chapel. One day when I was in its sacristy, a finely dressed woman—I'd say she was in her late fifties—entered, seeming to want to speak with me.

"Traditionally, when a new priest arrives, I give him something; I want you to have this memento of your stay at Saint Anthony's."

It was a $5 gold coin, something you didn't see every day. Never had I seen that lady before, or since. I've misplaced the coin more than once, and every time I lost it, something would happen to me. I don't know what to make of it. I've wondered who she was, and whether our encounter foreshadowed my work in the Church.

Whenever I had a free Sunday, I'd help out in a parish, be it Saint Clare of Assisi's (in the Bronx) during my years with

Bishop Sheen; Saint Jude's in Rockville, Maryland (in the Archdiocese of Washington, DC), while stationed at the Apostolic Delegation; or, during my Vatican years, at the Parrocchia del Sacro Cuore in Ciampino on Rome's outskirts.

I enjoyed parish life, but I wanted to understand the wider society my flock lived and worked in. And so, as previously mentioned, I embarked on the study of sociology at Fordham. It had one of the two best sociology departments in the country. (Columbia had the other.) There I met the man who sparked in me a love for the subject.

The Reverend Joseph P. Fitzpatrick, SJ, founded Fordham's Department of Sociology and Anthropology in 1959 and served as its first chairman. He was *the* expert on Puerto Rican immigration, a timely topic for any scholar who taught in the Bronx, which had, and still has, the highest concentration of Puerto Ricans in the United States. When I expressed my interest in the concept of liberty in Fascist Italy and the Constitution of the United States, he gave me the green light. For my dissertation topic, however, I focused on racial segregation, then headline news. To understand it, however, I had to experience it. The month I had spent helping out in a Harlem parish wouldn't do. I wanted to go deeper.

One summer during my years of study (from 1959 to 1961; I defended my dissertation in 1962), my uncle (the *other* "Father Franco") drove with me through 13 states in the South. My brief Harlem experience hardly prepared me for the regime of legalized racial segregation I was about to enter. For this New Yorker it was like visiting another planet.

In New Orleans, city buses were segregated. Dressed in civvies, I boarded a bus, moved to the rear, sat down, and pretended to read a newspaper. The driver growled in my direction:

"Hey, you!"

I continued "reading."

"I think he's talking to you," the guy next to me deduced.

"Yes, sir . . . what can I do for you?"

"That's not your place!"

"Maybe not . . . but it's all right."

"Hey, you! You here to give us problems?"

"No . . . ?"

"You from up North . . . I can tell!"

"Yeah, I am."

"I'm telling ya . . . That's not your place!"

Rather than giving him a win, I got off the bus. I sensed that unfriendly people were tailing me. By the grace of God, though, nothing happened. (I was a good runner, but glad I didn't have to prove it that day.)

I wore my collar in Chattanooga, Tennessee, where my uncle and I were looking for a place to stay for the night. There was no vacancy at the first motel we tried or at other facilities. At last we found one with a lit vacancy sign.

"We need a room for the night."

"No!" the receptionist shot back.

"You're from the North!"

"I am."

"Well, there's no room for you."

The Supreme Court hadn't yet outlawed discrimination in public accommodations. For that we had to wait until 1964, a few years in the future.

"Is that a phone?" I asked rhetorically. "I'm going to call the police. Your sign reads 'Vacancy.' You have to give us a room."

"So, you are here to bring problems . . . All right."

Her unforgettable words of surrender trailed off.

I was too anxious to sleep; flashbacks of documentaries on the segregated South filled my consciousness. We hit the road at dawn. Exhausted from my sleepless night, I dozed off behind the wheel. Uncle Ilario startled me awake in time to avoid our landing in a ditch.

⌒⊚⊚⌒

Back home, I continued balancing my studies at Fordham with my work with Bishop Sheen. I was transferred to Saint Dominic's on Unionport Road in the Bronx's Van Nest neighborhood for a couple of years, two stops from Fordham on the elevated train. Italian marble was used in Saint Dominic's construction in 1927, thanks to its pastor, Monsignor Dominic Fiorentino, an Italian marble aficionado. Assisting him were Father Joseph Raimondo, Father Joseph Adamo, and now me, the kid. I'd often take duty for one or another of these priests. Being on duty meant one couldn't move from the parish, but since filling in gifted me with study time, I welcomed every chance I got to sub for them.

Soon, however, my horizons would expand beyond anything I could have expected.

FIVE

Fulton J. Sheen and the Vatican Council

*Of all human activities,
man's listening to God is the supreme act
of his reasoning and will.*

POPE PAUL VI

Before setting foot in the seminary, I had read virtually every word Fulton J. Sheen ever published; and *Life Is Worth Living*, his weekly TV show, which aired from 1952 to 1957, was my "appointment television." I glimpsed him in May 1954 at the canonization of Pius X, whose body was carried through Saint Peter's Basilica, a most solemn event.* As the faithful thronged in a procession in Saint Peter's Square, they chanted to the reigning pontiff, Pius XII:

> *"Facciamo santo anche te!"* ("We will make you a saint as well!")

Having yet a year to go before ordination, I naturally tried to identify potential "stars" of the American hierarchy in the procession. Topping that list was Bishop Sheen. Yes, I saw

---

* Saint Pius X (1835–1914) was the Great War's first victim. He had done what he could to prevent it; he died of a broken heart as the Guns of August inaugurated the carnage.

American cardinals there, including Francis Spellman,* but Sheen was Sheen, impeccably outfitted.

Among Sheen's books, a favorite of mine is the one about the Blessed Mother, *The World's First Love*. Another is *Communism and the Conscience of the West*. They provided windows into two worlds, the one whence he came, the other whither he was going. I did not then know that they had prepared me to assist their author.

In the summer of 1959, during my summer appointment at Our Lady of Mount Carmel (OLMC), I was so taken by Sheen's personality and compelling presentation of Catholic doctrine that a crazy idea dawned on me.

Why couldn't I meet him?

Did I not qualify as one of his biggest fans? I had questions worth asking. But for me to entertain interviewing Fulton J. Sheen at the apex of his popularity took exceptional naïveté, if not (if I may trade in French for Yiddish) chutzpah. Yet the thought persisted, irresistibly. Why not? "I'm a priest; he's an auxiliary bishop."

Pushing past any lingering inhibitions, I convinced myself to make the call. It was easy to find the number of the National Director of the Society of the Propagation of the Faith in the phone book.

I dialed it from the parish. When a young lady answered, I announced:

---

* During Pius XII's reign (1939–1958), only two consistories were held to nominate members to the College of Cardinals. In the first, held in 1946 right after the Second World War, Archbishop Francis Spellman was given the cardinal's *biretta*; Angelo Giuseppe Roncalli's turn came during the second consistory in 1953.

"I'm a priest of the Archdiocese of New York, and I'd like to see Bishop Sheen. I've read his books and have some questions for him."

Edythe Brownett, God rest her soul, would become my friend. Years later, she confessed she didn't know at first what to tell me. Even heads of state would have to wait to be received by Fulton Sheen.

"Well, Father, I'll have to ask the bishop."

I waited for her return.

"How about tomorrow at 3:00 p.m.?"

This was normal, I thought. It wasn't.

Hopping the train to Manhattan, I dashed to the address Edythe supplied: 366 Fifth Avenue (the site of my future office). The elevator zoomed me to 12. I was ushered in.

"The bishop will see you for 15 minutes."

Rising from the chair behind his desk, he approached me.

"Yes, Father. . . Hello. . . Sit down."

He wasn't as tall as he appeared to be on television. He was of normal height.

My quarter hour began. His piercing, deep-set blue eyes bored holes in me; my questions got one-syllable replies.

"That's it? That's all Bishop Sheen has to say?" I thought, not realizing that 43 minutes had flown by.

After removing from a bookshelf a copy of *The Life of Christ*, one of his recent publications, he began to inscribe:

To Father . . .

"What's your name again?"

I provided it.

> To Father Hilario Franco
> In tribute to a good and learned priest,
> with fraternal esteem.
> Fulton J. Sheen.
> August 29, 1959

As he handed me the book (cherished to this day), he asked:

"What are you doing for lunch tomorrow?"

"Your Excellency, as a parish priest I'll have to ask my superior. Today happens to be my day off."

"All right. Ask him. Tomorrow, 12:30 p.m., 109 East 38th Street."

I couldn't get back to the Bronx fast enough. I went straight to Bishop Pernicone.

"Bishop," I began, "Fulton Sheen invited me to lunch tomorrow at his residence. May I have your permission to accept?"

Pernicone—a saintly man—exploded.

"Sit down, young man!"

I complied.

"Yes, you've done this and that, and you have a doctorate. But that's no excuse! Never lie to your superiors! Ever!"

My quick examination of conscience turned up no lie.

Bishop Pernicone continued:

"I'm an Auxiliary Bishop of New York. I see Bishop Sheen at these splendid dinners. But I've never so much as had tea with him!

I'm supposed to believe he invited you to lunch? If you had just asked permission to go out for lunch, I'd have given it!"

"Bishop, may I go out for lunch tomorrow?"

"All right!"

Years later Pernicone visited the Apostolic Delegation in Washington:

"You know, Hilary, for a long time I just didn't believe you."

I took the train the next day; this time my destination was 109 East 38th Street in Manhattan's Murray Hill section. I climbed the brownstone's six steps and rang the bell. I was greeted by Frederick, the cook. A Norwegian Lutheran, he had been so taken by Bishop Sheen that he left the service of Broadway impresario Billy Rose to serve the bishop. Frederick gestured to the downstairs dining room.

Over the years I'd see writers, artists, actors, and actresses fill that room. But Sheen's heart also went out to outcasts like Victor Anderson, a leper whose family could not tolerate his appearance. Sheen regularly invited Victor to dine with us and even provided him an apartment.

To illustrate the cover of *The Life of Christ*, Salvador Dalí had given Sheen permission to use the image of his masterpiece *Christ of Saint John of the Cross*. And one day—lo!—there was the great surrealist with his wife. This kid from Belmont was rubbing shoulders with these artistic geniuses and gifted conversationalists.

After dinner, we ascended the stairs to the main floor, and after a brief visit to the Blessed Sacrament in the chapel, our guests left. I was ready to do the same when Bishop Sheen turned to me.

"Father, can you stay with me another 15, 20 minutes?"

"Of course!"

"The Holy Father has named me a member of several antipreparatory commissions for the Council that he announced on January 25th, namely, for the Laity, Missions, and Communications." *

Eventually, the bishop would be named a member of subsequent preparatory commissions as well as of the Council's proper commissions. By the "Council" he meant, of course, the Second Vatican Council. Political upheaval in Rome in 1870 prevented the First Vatican Council from being formally concluded. The convening of a new council automatically closes its predecessor, and that's what convening Vatican II did for Vatican I.

Taking the name John, Angelo Cardinal Roncalli had been elected pope on October 28, 1958. Three months later, on January 25, 1959, he announced in the Basilica of Saint Paul Outside the Walls his desire that his pontificate achieve three things.

The first was to convene a new Synod of the Diocese of Rome. It had been a long time since the last one, and after all, he was the Bishop of Rome.

Second was to update the Code of Canon Law. Things had changed since 1917, the year of its last revision. This would touch the life of the whole Church. As many of the cardinals present in the basilica were canon lawyers, this project raised no eyebrows.

---

* Some of you may think you caught a typo. Yes, the prefix "anti-" means "against" and "ante-" means "before." Nevertheless, the official Vatican documents show "anti-," not "ante-." See, for example, Vincenzo Carbone, "Vatican Council II: Light for the Church and the Modern World," *Tertium Millennium*, No. 2, May 1997, http://www.vatican.va/jubilee_2000/magazine/documents/ju_mag_01051997_p-21_en.html. Blame it on the evolution of Latin and Italian or whatever. The commissions to which Sheen was named were antipreparatory.

But then came the third goal: We prayed to the Holy Spirit and had the inspiration to convene an ecumenical council for the Church.

Well, that came as a great surprise, even a shock, to the cardinals present (most of them, cardinals of the Roman Curia). Not all were enthusiastic. Maybe none were. To say that meeting all three goals would involve a lot of work would understate things.

As for the commissions Sheen referred to, one was the Commission on the Missions, a natural consideration, given his directorship of the Society for the Propagation of the Faith in the USA. Sheen continued:

"I was wondering . . . since you have a degree in biblical theology and know languages . . . could you help me?"

It took a millisecond for me to answer:

"Of course, Bishop!"

The papal announcement had occurred eight months earlier, so by August things were getting under way, and that's when he asked this kid for help in preparing for the Council. I began helping him in my time off; once I was named Sheen's assistant—and his *peritus* (expert)—this work became time *on.*

As mentioned, for two years I had been assigned to Saint Dominic's while studying for my degree in sociology, and then to Assumption parish in New Brighton, Staten Island, where I'd spend three-plus years. The Right Reverend Monsignor Charles Rizzo, God rest his soul, was the pastor. He was not pleased to learn of my conciliar assignment.

"Call the cardinal tomorrow! Tell him you're not accepting!"

The parish had another assistant pastor, but Monsignor Rizzo depended on me for most of the parish work, including the needs of Catholics in a nearby hospital (then named Staten Island Hospital) and the parish's youth activities.* For my appointment as Bishop Sheen's assistant, however, there was another dimension: Monsignor Rizzo and his sister were friends of Cardinal Alfredo Ottaviani, who had offered them seats for the Council's solemn opening!† Someone had to watch the shop. I was "volunteered."

"You can't leave me now!" he insisted.

"Monsignor, I always obey my superior's directives, but I won't be saying no to Bishop Sheen."

For him to accept this reality it took a call from Cardinal Spellman's office.

Many in the press were of the opinion that Pope John XXIII, 77 years old at the time of his election, would be a "transitional pope," not a transformational one. But Angelo Giuseppe Roncalli, under the Providence of God, had other plans.

Believing he was acting on an impulse from the Holy Spirit, he took his office seriously. A profound grasp of the faith grounded the pastoral simplicity for which he was known and loved. A veteran of the Vatican's diplomatic corps, he wasn't reared to be a diplomat. He was not a graduate of the Accademia Ecclesiastica as was Pius XII, who had served in

---

* Among other things, I arranged Friday night parish dances that attracted hundreds of youngsters from all over Staten Island. For one of them I hired Chubby Checker of "Let's do the twist" fame.

† Cardinal Alfredo Ottaviani (1890–1979), one of the Council's leading conservative voices, served as Secretary of the Holy Office from 1959 to 1966, which was reorganized as the Congregation for the Doctrine of the Faith. He served as this dicastery's Pro-Prefect until 1968.

the Secretariat of State in several roles before becoming Pius XII's Secretary of State.

One pope presided over the First Council of the Vatican (1869–1870); two pontiffs over the Second (1962–1965). The former lasted 10 months, and representatives came from a relatively few countries; the latter lasted three months of each of its three years, and it hosted 2,525 Fathers from the world over, two-thirds of them non-Europeans. Whereas Vatican I had been inward-looking, Vatican II, more extroverted in orientation, was animated by a generous idea of the Church's role in the world, whose problems in the early 1960s were hardly confined to doctrinal issues.

The unification of Italy had constrained the circumstances under which Pius IX convened and guided Vatican I; the so-called "conquest of Rome" in 1870 forced him to send everyone home before he could formally close it. One of the Council's lasting results was the definition of the dogma of papal infallibility *ex cathedra*. Before papal infallibility was defined as a dogma, however, Pius IX had invoked it in 1854 when he defined the Immaculate Conception of Mary as a dogma to be believed by the faithful. Almost a century later, on November 1st of the Jubilee Year of 1950, Pius XII invoked papal infallibility to define another Marian dogma, the Assumption of the Blessed Virgin Mary.*

Il Papa Buono, as the faithful affectionately referred to Saint Pope John XXIII, died on June 3, 1963. It was one of the two times that year that I cried. As a young priest still finding his

---

* About this teaching, a former theology professor of mine initially had doubts, but on the day the pope proclaimed it, he told me: "I have prayed and now firmly believe in the new dogma of the Assumption of the Blessed Mother."

way around the Church and the world, I knew Roncalli was an elderly man whom the Lord might call to be with Him sooner rather than later. Nevertheless, I made my way to a church to ask God why He had permitted that to happen in the middle of the great Council convened by the "Papa Buono" Pope John had set the Council in motion, but was not permitted to see it through to the end.

Roncalli had been the apostolic delegate in Bulgaria. When later named to that position in Turkey, he forged certificates of baptism to save Jewish lives. As an ambassador of the Holy See, he knew non-Catholic countries firsthand; he *felt*, not just intellectually grasped, their potential for evangelization. His vision for the Church was that of an inclusive macrocosm of humanity. He broadened Her horizons, opening Her arms, if I may borrow Fulton J. Sheen's simile, like Bernini's fleshly columns and embracing the world. For the first time, bishops from the Third World would take part in making needed changes.

The Council's sessions didn't consume the calendar year, convening during September, October, and November. The conclave that elected John XXIII's successor met when the Council was not in session. On June 21st, the Feast of the Sacred Heart, we witnessed the election of Giovanni Battista Montini, then Archbishop of Milan. He had been Pro-Secretary of State under Pius XII (along with Domenico Tardini, later on to become Cardinal Tardini and John XXIII's Secretary of State).

Pius XII was rumored to have said, "I don't need secretaries of state." Montini and Tardini were jointly Pro-Secretaries of State, but not archbishops or cardinals. Montini became

Archbishop of Milan because, it was said, Pius XII wanted the diplomat to have had pastoral experience. And so he was sent to Milan, where he did an exceptional job there in a short time. When the newly elected Pope John XXIII decided to hold a consistory to name new cardinals, Montini's name topped the list.

When he was elected pope, Montini took the name of Paul, after the Apostle. He wanted to continue the series of pontiffs who had borne that name. There hadn't been a pope named Paul in almost 350 years.

In those days, the four-century-old informal tradition that the pope "had" to be an Italian still held. Besides his wonderful work as Pro-Secretary of State and archbishop, Montini had long Vatican experience from the time he was a young priest. "We have the right man," it was thought. The transition to the new pontificate in the midst of a Council was, all things considered, smooth.

Paul VI was the man to carry through John XXIII's vision. He had served two popes, been a confidant of Pius XII, and served as archbishop in one of the largest dioceses. He had the requisite education and experience. Paul could have decided against reconvening the Council, but instead became its leader. John had led it from October 11, 1962, to the day he died the following June; Paul conducted most of the Council from its second session until the solemn closing on December 8, 1965.

One signature move of the new pontiff was to divest his office of triumphal vestments and other expressions of a bygone age, which, as I noted earlier, carried the risk of spiritual and social tone-deafness. These included the cardinals' long trains and other Renaissance-era vestiges like the *sedia gestatoria*, the ornate ceremonial chair for carrying the pope, and the papal tiara, or *triregnum*, representing three kingdoms (father of kings, governor of the world, and Vicar of Christ). These insignia survived only the beginning of Paul VI's pontificate.

The people of Milan had gifted the tiara to him, but in keeping with the Council's spirit, he sold it, donating the proceeds to charity.* The Milanese accepted his new style. The transition was as courageous as it was smooth: a weaker man would have declined to shoulder the Council's burden. "No, we are going to continue," he vowed.

The period between papacies is called *sede vacante*, "the chair is vacant." That is, no one during this period occupies the Chair of the Apostle Peter. Until a new pope is elected, there is no authority to undertake anything significant. The Church's governance is, if you will, in suspended animation: we have to wait until the new pope announces his plans. The wisdom of 2,000 years of Church history counsels patience and waiting.

As anyone who reads their pronouncements can discern, Pope Benedict XVI and Pope Francis represent different styles. Bishop Fulton J. Sheen never liked to sort churchmen into "conservative" or "liberal" bins. There are no conservatives and liberals in the Church. We might have different opinions, but they're always expressed *within* the context of the Church's mission. As long as the value of Her unity is kept front-and-center, no schism threatens. History shows that schism is usually the result of secular political interference, not religious disaffection.

---

* The American Catholics who bought it arranged to have it displayed in the Basilica of the National Shrine of the Immaculate Conception in Washington, DC.

ఆర్థిక

October 11, 1962, the day Saint Pope John XXIII opened the Second Vatican Council, and not his earthly or heavenly birthday, would become his feast day. He said the Council should be an *aggiornamento*, an updating of the Church. He probably had this idea from when he was the apostolic delegate in Bulgaria in the early 1930s, long before becoming nuncio to Paris.

Roncalli hadn't enjoyed the confidence of Domenico Tardini, Pius XII's Pro-Secretary of State; yet later on John XXIII would ask Tardini to be his Secretary of State. When it was time to name the first cardinals of John XXIII's pontificate, Tardini handed the Holy Father a list of possible candidates. As the story has come to me, the back-and-forth between these men went something like this:

"Your Holiness, I know the limit is 70, but three others should be considered."

"Who decided on 70?"

"Sixtus V."

"Was he a pope?"

"Yes. A great one."

"Am I pope?"

"Yes, Your Holiness."

"Well, then, let's set aside the number 70. And we're going to make cardinals of these three as well."

Taking the list, the pope added another name: Domenico Tardini!

History does have its beautiful moments.

SIX

The Council's Mission: Updating the Church

Each of us is the result of a thought of God.
Each of us is willed. Each of us is loved.
Each of us is necessary.

POPE BENEDICT XVI

The Second Vatican Council's Fathers, including Bishop Sheen, arrived in Rome a few days before October 11, 1962, to get settled in. Initially, he took lodging at the Hotel Eden, but for the last sessions we stayed at the brand-new Cavalieri Hilton Hotel,* which Conrad Hilton envisioned as "a balcony on Rome." Built on Monte Mario, it has a splendid view that rivals that of the Pincio Promenade in the Villa Borghese Gardens. The Hilton International's vice-president, Robert Quain, an admirer of Sheen, arranged for 78 American bishops to stay there.

While on a bus heading to the Council one day, Bishop Sheen asked why, with so many bishops in this hotel, there was no place in the hotel to reserve for the Blessed Sacrament. The bishops could say Mass in their hotel rooms, but not spend time before the Blessed Sacrament. Sheen was accustomed to his daily Holy Hour.

---

* It's now advertised as the Rome Cavalieri, a Waldorf Astoria Hotel. For a contemporary artistic rendering, see page 18 of the Hilton Annual Report for 1962, https://ir.hilton.com/~/media/Files/H/HiltonWorldwide-IR-V3/annual-report/1962-Annual-Report.pdf.

"Father Franco, please get us a room for this."

I convinced the hotel manager to let us use one that flanked the lobby; then I bought materials needed to transform it into a chapel.

As a graduate of Pontifical Roman Seminary, the world's premier seminary, I was delighted to hear that John XXIII had named Pericle Felici, recently consecrated archbishop, as General Secretary of the Second Vatican Council. Felici was a Latinist, theologian, and judge of the Sacred Rota. (Everything was done in Latin, but without simultaneous translation.) Responsibility for the Council's organization and smooth running fell on Felici's shoulders.

Delighted, I say, because not only was Pericle Felici a fellow alumnus, but he had also been its spiritual director when I was there.* That made it easy for me to get needed information from the General Secretariat. One of my former classmates, Mariano De Nicolò (a future bishop) had become Felici's secretary. Father De Nicolò was also a terrific source.

If the pope was the Council's director, Felici was its producer. Felici had a big job, and it was my privilege to assist him with some details. His office corresponded with the Council Fathers, rendering the pope's intentions into practical plans. But the pope didn't hurry his decision-making.

Toward the end of 1959, anticipation of the Council surfaced in the press. Everybody, certainly every Catholic, wanted to know what was going to be discussed. The Fathers, bishops, were coming from north and south, east and west. Most of them, including our American bishops, didn't know Latin (or

---

* At the Council's end, Pope Paul VI created Felici a cardinal and invited him to join him in his 1965 visit to the United States.

Italian, for that matter). They came with considerable pastoral and administrative experience from their schools and parishes, but their competency in theology varied widely. They were faithful to the magisterium, the Church's teaching authority, but few were interested in delving into theology and canon law.

The novelty of being in the Vatican during the Council never wore off, even after a couple of years. Each session had its own character and freshness. The proposals of the Council Fathers gave expression to many of the issues Bishop Sheen and I had debated over meals and during our hours of preparatory work. Crowding ourselves into one or another coffee bar (located inside Saint Peter's Basilica and on both sides of its main nave), we argued Council matters over cappuccinos and brioches. Regular patrons nicknamed one of them the "Bar Jonah."

If I remember correctly, the only time all the Council Fathers raced from the coffee bars to their seats was when they heard Bishop Sheen's name announced: *"Audiamus Excellentissimum ac Reverendissimum Dominum, Dominum Fulton J. Sheen."* ("We shall now hear the Most Excellent and Reverend Bishop, Bishop Fulton J. Sheen.") He held them spellbound, living up to his reputation!

It took an army of workers to construct and maintain the Council's infrastructure. Everything had to be perfect. Meetings were held every morning and broke up around 12:30. The Fathers might then take in the sights, but from four o'clock on they attended *circuli minores* ("minor circles"). Meanwhile, the Vatican gardens had to be manicured. The great number of Council Fathers didn't include their entourages of *periti* and advisors.

The one venue spacious enough to accommodate all 2,625 men was the main nave of Saint Peter's Basilica. Each morning the Council would start with the liturgy of the day. Masses in different rites were organized, not only the Roman, but also the Ambrosian, the Mozarabic, the Carthusian, the Malabaric, the Armenian, and the Rite of Braga. Occasionally an African rhythm, punctuated by the pounding of benches, suffused the basilica. We denizens of the twenty-first century must remember that only "First World" bishops participated in Vatican I, but the "Third World" provided Vatican II with two-thirds of its Fathers.

The debates were well-run, and Council presidents (mostly cardinals) took turns directing them. Each Council Father had to submit in advance the text of his "intervention" (his contribution to the debate) to the General Secretariat. When his time came, he'd be given 10 minutes.

In the caverns of my memory the booming voice of the Cardinal President, Archbishop of Munich Cardinal Julius Döpfner, still echoes. He'd preface his announcement of the prospective speaker's name with:

"Audiamus Reverendissimum et Excellentissimum Dominum, Dominum _____.*"* ("We hear the Most Reverend and Excellent Bishop, Bishop _____.")

Cardinal Döpfner would rein in loquacious Italian- and Spanish-speaking bishops who, brandishing their fluency in Latin, tended to go over the allotted time:

"Tempus tuum exhaustum est! Valeas concludere!" ("Your time is up! Conclude!")

When the day's debates concluded (around 12:30 p.m.), thousands of red-cassocked Council Fathers exited the basilica to catch rides outside the Bernini colonnade. They lunched in their residence, and then, as I noted earlier, around four o'clock they formed *circuli minores* with their *periti* and advisors to review the day's topics. These might go on until late in the evening.

I remember the day Karol Wojtyła, the future Pope (and Saint) John Paul II, arrived at the Council as a young auxiliary bishop from Krakow, Poland. His successor, Pope Benedict XVI, was then simply Father Joseph Ratzinger, one of many expert theologians in attendance. His official role was theological consultant to Cologne's Archbishop Cardinal Josef Frings, a Council president (one of 10). Now famous for his defense of Catholic orthodoxy, Father Ratzinger was viewed as a reformer, on friendly terms with controversial theologians like Hans Küng and Edward Schillebeeckx. Father Ratzinger needed a permit to attend the Council's sessions, as did every consultant. (For security reasons, our cars had to display a special pass as we drove through Vatican City.)

Father Ratzinger and I met for the preparation of *Ad gentes*, the conciliar decree on the Missionary Activity of the Church (published December 7, 1965). He was impressed with Bishop Fulton J. Sheen, another member of this preparatory commission, the man who brought me to the Council. Toward the end of Benedict's pontificate, he paid a visit to the Società del Verbo Divino (Society of the Divine Word, the Verbites) in Nemi (not far from Castel Gandolfo, the pope's summer residence). He recalled Sheen's mesmerizing interventions:

I am truly grateful for the possibility to see this house in Nemi once again after 47 years. I have a very beautiful memory of it, perhaps the most beautiful of the entire Council. I lived in the centre of Rome, at the College of Santa Maria dell'Anima, with all that noise: it was also beautiful! But being here in a green space, having this breath of nature and fresh air as well, was just beautiful in itself. And then there was the company of so many great theologians, with the fine and important task of drafting a *Decree on Mission* [*Ad gentes*]. I remember first of all the Superior General [of the Verbites] at that time, Fr. Schütte,* who had suffered in China, and had been condemned, then expelled. He was full of missionary dynamism, of the need to give the missionary spirit a new impetus. And he had me invited, a very young theologian of no importance, I don't know why. But it was a great gift for me.

Then there was Fulton Sheen, who kept us enthralled in the evening with his tales, Fr. Congar and the great missiologists of Louvain. For me it was a spiritual enrichment, a great gift.†

Years later when I worked in the Vatican, I'd walk past Joseph Ratzinger every morning: as Cardinal Prefect of the Congregation for the Doctrine of the Faith (CDF), he crossed Saint Peter's Square from his apartment on Piazza Città Leonina

---

* Father Johannes Schütte (1913-1971), theologian of missions.

† "Address of His Holiness Benedict XVI," visit to the "Ad Gentes" House of the Verbite Missionaries, Nemi, Italy, July 9, 2012, http://www.vatican.va/content/benedict-xvi/en/speeches/2012/july/documents/hf_ben-xvi_spe_20120709_nemi.html.

to his office at the Sant'Uffizio building. Always cordial, and nearly always sporting a black beret, he always had a kind word for youngish Vatican officials like me en route to our respective offices. This routine of 27 years was broken when, to his great surprise, he was elected pope in 2005. Not many months before that, Cardinal Ratzinger, then in his late seventies and a recent heart surgery patient, asked Pope John Paul II (himself afflicted with Parkinson's) to be allowed to retire in his Bavarian hometown of Marktl to study and write. The pope refused.

As Cardinal Prefect, Joseph Ratzinger focused on his doctrinal work, staying in his office except to give a lecture, and even then rarely outside the Eternal City. Apart from his participation in interdicasterial meetings, he didn't really know the Roman Curia. Thus, when he became pope, he was initially at a loss to name people he'd need to work with. In due course, Pope Benedict named his former CDF Secretary, Cardinal Tarcisio Bertone, his new Secretary of State, and San Francisco Archbishop William J. Levada to succeed him at the CDF. Cardinal Levada used to be an official there; as its new prefect, he'd serve in the highest curial post an American ever held.

Benedict was also comfortable with two American presidential administrations: George W. Bush was openly a fan of Benedict's,* and Barack Obama received him with great flourish during his 2008 trip to America.

---

* Benedict's saintly predecessor, John Paul II, unsuccessfully appealed to President George H. W. Bush, in a letter presented by his envoy, Cardinal Pio Laghi (former nuncio to the United States, 1984–1990), asking him not to commit the country to the Iraq War, which he nevertheless did on March 15, 2003.

When it came to eating during the Council, we were on our own. With other American bishops, Archbishop Sheen and I would board a bus back to the Hilton, drop off papers, stop at a hotel restaurant, take counter seats, and order—as Sheen would articulate with great deliberation—*uova strapazzate*, scrambled eggs. (Years later, I had the privilege of blessing the wedding of a waitress there, Teresa, who used to serve us scrambled eggs.) Many moons in the future, after Sheen retired from Rochester, he lived in an apartment in the Pavilion (500 East 77th Street in Manhattan). Whenever I'd visit him, he'd don an apron, turn to me, and say:

"Uova strapazzate?"

Monsignor Pio Laghi was stationed in India as a member of the Vatican's diplomatic corps. In 1980, as Archbishop, Pio Laghi was named Apostolic Delegate to the United States. In 1984, he became the first Nuncio of the Holy See to the United States when, under President Reagan, the Vatican would at last have full diplomatic relationships with my country.* A nun had impressed the young Laghi during his Indian assignment. He approached me with a question for Bishop Sheen:†

"A nun from India is coming to Rome with her sisters to work with the homeless. Could Bishop Sheen meet with her?"

---

* Former New York Mayor Robert Wagner once served as the representative of the president to the pope, but William Wilson, a close friend of Reagan's, was the first ambassador of the United States to the Vatican.

† Laghi was my elder, but as we were Pontifical Roman Seminary alumni, his running this request by me made sense.

I thought he could. Bishop Sheen would take the time to see the people I suggested. He agreed to meet with Anjezë Gonxhe Bojaxhiu, a then-obscure sister who took the name Mary Teresa and whom the world would come to know as Mother, and now Saint, Teresa of Calcutta.

During the Council, Bishop Sheen was invited to give talks in several places. One unforgettable speech was to an overflow audience in the Teatro del Palazzo Reale in Naples, and I served as simultaneous translator. But making speeches before VIPs in luxurious settings wasn't his goal; preaching the truth was. At the proverbial drop of a hat, he'd travel to the slums to find out what its inhabitants needed.

So, not long after Monsignor Laghi's feeler, we accepted the invitation to see Mother Teresa in Tor Fiscale, where the *baraccati* (slum dwellers) lived along the New Appian Way. No GPS then, but still we found the humble structure, little better than a shack. There were no chairs; the sisters sat on crossed legs. Embarrassed, the sisters borrowed something for us to sit on from another hovel, but Bishop Sheen didn't care to sit when he talked. He stood for this meeting.

Miss Bojaxhiu knew him by reputation, of course, but had also read his books and heard him speak. Now his personal presence came into play. Though a native Albanian, Miss Bojaxhiu spoke good English. As a young lady she had gone to Ireland to join the Sisters of Loreto, and they sent her to New Delhi, India, to teach at a prestigious high school. One day on the way to Darjeeling, she took a train outside the school's walls and was almost overcome by the heartrending poverty. Teresa was never the same after that trip.

When I deal with people of her and Bishop Sheen's spiritual caliber, I feel something extraordinary to which words cannot do justice. Sheen's piercing eyes would penetrate the marrow of your soul. Mother Teresa's charisma, and her face's distinctive wrinkles (then already forming), conveyed an almost palpable strength, power, and determination. I only wish I had taken more advantage of the opportunity that knowing them offered. Remembering this on the anniversary of my ordination, I meditate on the fleeting years. Permission to contemplate life's transitoriness while we're immersed in it is one we rarely grant ourselves.

Our meeting with Mother Teresa and her nuns lasted about two hours. The work of the Council beckoned. In the car Bishop Sheen turned to me:

"This is a truly wonderful and saintly lady."

Bishop Sheen perceived her saintliness. Her sense of life moved him, as it had Monsignor Laghi. The meeting must have influenced Bishop Sheen's speech to the Council on the Missions on November 9, 1964, the one that, when it was announced, emptied Bar Jonah:

Paul VI, reigning as a missionary pontiff, has suggested to the council that our schema be polished and developed. Let us do this, at the same time granting to every member of the commission the right to choose his own expert . . . In place of the theological question *What* are Missions?, I would suggest that we turn to the practical question: *Where* are the Missions? Are the Missions exclusively in those territories where there are non-Christians? Or are the Missions also in those regions, where there are few priests, few churches and great poverty? The simple answer to this question is: The Missions are both. . . .

We bishops in this Council must not enter into a dispute about what is a missionary territory and what is not, or who belongs to this congregation or to that congregation, saying: "I am one of Paul's men," "I am one of Apollo's," or "I am one of Cephas"; while someone else says "I owe my faith to Christ alone." What are you saying? Is there more than one Christ? (1 Cor. 1:12).

Let us not be like the priest and the Levite in the parable of the Good Samaritan, who passed by the wounded man saying: "He does not belong to our congregation" . . .

In the Body of Christ there are no "new churches," there are no "old churches," for we are all living cells in that Body dependent on one another. One of the conciliar Fathers has asked that all reference to poverty be taken out of this schema. I beg you most earnestly, Venerable Fathers, that the notion of poverty be strongly affirmed in this Council.

Put your finger on the 30th Parallel; run it around a globe of the earth, lifting it slightly above China. What do you find?

Practically all of the prosperity is above the 30th Parallel, and the greater part of the poverty of the world is beneath the 30th Parallel, that is in Africa, Asia and Latin America.

And now his central point:

> As chastity was the fruit of the Council of Trent, and obedience the fruit of the First Vatican Council, so may the spirit of poverty be the fruit of this Second Vatican Council.
>
> We live in a world in which 200 million people would willingly take the vow of poverty tomorrow, if they could live as well, eat as well, be clothed as well, and be housed as well as I am—or even some who take the vow of poverty.
>
> The greater number of bishops in this Council is living in want or in persecution, and they come from all peoples and all nations.
>
> As only a wounded Christ could convert a doubting Thomas, so only a Church wounded by poverty can convert a doubting world.

Mother Teresa's life supplied one vector of Bishop Sheen's thinking on poverty, but it wasn't the only one. We had traveled to Thailand together. We'd visited leper colonies. We even visited Calcutta (now known as Kolkata) but, oddly, not to see her.

One day years later when Mother was in New York, Bishop Sheen received her at the Fifth Avenue headquarters of the Society for the Propagation of the Faith. Every afternoon at three o'clock, we'd say the Rosary, using the missionary rosary the bishop had designed, which sported beads of different colors for different continents. Here was the now world-famous

Mother Teresa praying the Rosary with us. She had become a great advocate for that "spiritual weapon."

When Mother Teresa visited me in my Vatican office years later, her face was no longer unfamiliar. In those days, responsibility for approving statutes for lay movements or for dealing with them (e.g., Communion and Liberation, the Neocatechumenal Way) was a competency for my dicastery (since then assigned to other dicasteries). Mother, accompanied by two sisters, more than once came to discuss statutes for the male counterpart of her Missionaries of Charity. At one point I had to leave to retrieve documents from my office. I returned to deafening silence: the sisters were in prayer, bent over their rosary beads.

I cherish a snapshot of Mother and me taken during her last visit to New York. (The cheap camera date-stamped it June 24, 1997.) The two of us were talking about her future projects, even though she was ill and wheelchair-bound. Saints are always on the go, despite advanced age or suffering! I suggested she go home to rest. The Lord called her Home a little more than two months later, September 5, 1997.

My connection to her didn't end there. Early in the new millennium's first year, 2001, I got a call from Sister Maria Nirmala Joshi, the congregation's new Superior General. She reminded me of the promise I made to Mother that I'd preach the retreat of the new millennium to sisters making their final profession of vows. If I remember correctly, there were more than 140 of them. Caught by surprise, I asked whether I was still bound by that promise, now that Mother was in Heaven.

Sister Nirmala reminded me that the sisters have a long memory.

"When is this scheduled? I hope not during Lent; I can't leave my parish."

"Oh no, it'll be at the end of April, beginning of May."

Relieved, I asked:

"Where?," and with great nonchalance she said:

"Oh, in Calcutta."

I had no choice. That April, I went to Cologne, Germany, to bless my nephew Stefano's wedding to a wonderful young lady named Daniela; then southward to Rome—en route to Kolkata (as it is now known), India! On every one of the next 10 days I gave four talks on spiritual direction for the sisters. I treasure my memory of that week-and-a-half, despite the heat (125 degrees Fahrenheit, plus ghastly humidity) and the limitation of my cuisine to white rice chased by Coca-Cola.

Every night I visited one or another of their ministry's sites. One time, their leper colony Shanti Nagar ("The Place of Peace"); another, a home for abandoned babies; then Nirmal Hriday ("Home of the Pure Heart"), the former Hindu temple dedicated to the goddess Kali, once gifted to Mother and renamed (and repurposed as) Mother Teresa's Home for the Dying Destitutes in Kalighat, Kolkata. In Kalighat, those about to breathe their last in Kolkata's streets are washed and cleaned before leaving this world. "A beautiful death for people who lived like animals," Mother used to say, "is for them to die like angels, loved and wanted." In such a congested and noisy city, I was impressed that a room in this former Hindu temple is reserved for perpetual adoration of the Blessed Sacrament. Two sisters are continually there in adoration, undeterred by the street's unbearable cacophony. I was blessed to join them for a while.

A couple of months before the close of the Council in 1965, on October 4th to be exact, on the Feast of St. Francis, Pope Paul VI made a whirlwind trip to New York to address the UN General Assembly. In and out. It began at 8:00 in the morning and ended at 11:00 that evening. In those 15 hours the pope addressed the General Assembly, celebrated Mass at Yankee Stadium, and met with President Johnson at the Towers of the Waldorf Astoria.

Popes have always had to deal with history's flux, the Deposit of Faith's permanent things, and the interplay between the flux and the permanence. The secularizing times of Paul VI were no exception. Aristotle distinguished the "substance" of a thing (which makes it that kind of thing) from its "accidents" (which can change without making it a different kind of thing). The substance of the Church, her dogmas, for example, should never be touched, but the accidents can be and have been adapted to meet the level of our time. That's the *aggiornamento*, or updating, aimed at by John XXIII. It encompassed the Roman Synod, the revision of canon law (both long overdue), and, of course, the Council. The controversies we associate with the sixties (e.g., war and peace, the sexual revolution) were debated at the Council. One fruit of this debate was *Gaudium et Spes*—Joy and Hope—a conciliar document whose subject is the presence of the Church in the modern world.

Because everything was in Latin, American bishops had dif-
ficulty following Council documents. They celebrated Mass in
Latin, but weren't fluent in it as were, say, Cardinal Spellman
(the first American to have served in the Vatican's Secretariat
of State), Bishop John Joseph Wright of Pittsburgh, or James
Henry Griffiths, the Auxiliary Bishop of New York. Non-
Latinists therefore risked noticing the accidents at the expense
of the substance.

SEVEN

Movers and Shakers

Above all, don't fear difficult moments.
The best comes from them.

RITA LEVI-MONTALCINI, ITALIAN NOBEL LAUREATE

On December 9, 1979, I was working in my Vatican office when I got the news that Bishop Fulton J. Sheen, my mentor and friend, was called to the House of the Father at the age of 84. I made plans to fly to New York where, at Saint Patrick's Cathedral, I concelebrated his funeral Mass, the main celebrant being Cardinal Terence Cooke. Some of the celebrities in attendance had taken instruction from Bishop Sheen in preparation for entering the Church, among them, former congresswoman and ambassador Clare Boothe Luce. Another attendee was the evangelist Billy Graham, who deemed Sheen the greatest communicator of the twentieth century.

Memories float down the river of my mind, for instance (in no particular order):

Every Wednesday during Lent in 1966, Sheen and I took the New York's Midtown Tunnel into the borough of Queens (in the Brooklyn diocese) to Our Lady Queen of Martyrs, pastored by Auxiliary Bishop Joseph Denning. Lively dinners followed Sheen's preaching.

A few weeks after attending a Jewish memorial service in Riverdale for former New York Mayor Robert F. Wagner's secretary on March 22, 1966, Bishop Sheen began celebrating the *Novus Ordo Missae* (the New Order of the Mass) in English, something he was almost reluctant to do. The following month, on April 12, 1966, he and I completed the work we began on proposals for the revision of the Code of Canon Law, a goal of John XXIII. I sent it off to Rome.

Between 1959 and 1961, Haiti's dictator, François Duvalier, had expelled the archbishop of Port-au-Prince, the Jesuit order, and many priests. These predations earned him excommunication. On April 20, 1966, I went to JFK Airport on Bishop Sheen's behalf to greet Archbishop (later Cardinal) Antonio Samorè, number two in the Vatican's Secretariat of State. Samorè was en route to Haiti to restore relations and restart the Church's hierarchy there in the wake of the Duvalier era. A Haitian archbishop was named for the first time. I met Cardinal Samorè again many times when I was in Rome.

Not many know that Archbishop Sheen was an informal FBI friend. From time to time John Malone, head of the FBI's New York office during the tumultuous sixties and seventies, would join us for dinner.

For most people, I suppose May 13th, the 133rd day of the year, is just another day. But Catholics know it as the day in 1917 that Our Lady first appeared to the children at Fátima and, in 1983, that we almost lost Pope John Paul II to an assassin's bullet.

But there's another reason May 13th has a special place in my diary: in 1966 Archbishop Sheen had a 22-minute private audience with Pope Paul VI. Monsignor (later Cardinal) Loris Francesco Capovilla (John XXIII's secretary) introduced me to the pope in his antechamber, but the meeting between Paul VI and Sheen was just between them. I still have the rosary the Holy Father gave me after his private audience with Sheen.

Another church where Bishop Sheen was invited to preach was Saint Agnes near Grand Central Station in Manhattan. This strip of East 43rd Street (between Lexington and Third Avenues) was renamed "Archbishop Fulton J. Sheen Place" and dedicated on October 7, 1980, the Feast of the Holy Rosary. Then-Mayor Ed Koch noted that the area was "selected because it is the busiest pedestrian street in the world! ... Thus befitting the most famous churchman of our century." And it was from Saint Agnes's pulpit that his sermons were carried to the ends of the earth.

When Bishop Sheen preached the Three Hours on Good Friday in Saint Patrick's Cathedral, the surrounding streets were closed to traffic. The cathedral being filled to capacity, outdoor loudspeakers were set up. In one celebrated sermon, he contrasted the sculpture of Atlas directly across Fifth Avenue with the Cross inside the church. Here's how he rendered that meditation for *Our Grounds of Hope*:

> Opposite St. Patrick's Cathedral in New York is a giant statue of Atlas, bending and groaning and grunting under the weight of the world. That is modern man! The world is too much with him, late and soon. The world is too heavy for him and man is breaking under it, trying like a silly child to carry it alone, without any help or grace or faith from God.
>
> The other image I see is that of the God-Man on Good Friday, carrying a Cross, taking upon Himself the burden of others and proving that sacrifice for sin, selflessness and love of God and neighbor alone, can remake the world.
>
> No one will get out of this world without carrying some burden. Atlas will never get out from under that world; the Man Who carried the Cross will get out from under it, for it leads to Resurrection and a crown in Life

Eternal. This is the choice before us: either try to revolutionize the world and break under it or revolutionize ourselves and remake the world.

Marxism-Leninism—arguably the greatest ideological assault in the twentieth century on Christianity in general and on Catholicism in particular—doesn't merit mention, let alone condemnation, in the Second Vatican Council's documents. But neither does any other political system. The embrace of the world that Saint John XXIII promoted through the Council didn't allow for this negative note. He said, "I hate communism, but I love communists." I remember when, early in 1953, years before I met Bishop Sheen, he speculated on TV that something could happen to the Soviet leadership. Stalin died the following week. All men are mortal!

Fear of nuclear war hung in the air during the Council. One night Pope John XXIII privately received Aleksei Adzhubei, editor of *Izvestia* (the former Soviet Union's "paper of record"), and his wife, Rada—Soviet Premier Nikita Khrushchev's daughter. The pope offered to mediate between Khrushchev and Kennedy, raising the prospect of breaking the impasse without risk to their reputations.[*]

Pope John's encyclical *Pacem in Terris* was prepared, written, and published in the aftermath of the 1962 Cuban Missile Crisis and issued on April 11, 1963. His diplomatic

---

[*] I write this on the basis of information not publicly available. Contemporary reports show John XXIII and Adzhubei meeting in March 1963.

skill, honed over decades as nuncio to France and papal delegate to Bulgaria, Greece, and Turkey, led also to the release of Josyf Slipyj, Major Archbishop of Lviv, Ukraine (later to become cardinal) after 18 years of hard labor. A denizen of the Soviet's GULAG prison system since 1945, mostly in Siberia, Slipyj was ordered released by Khrushchev in January 1963. (I must register my surprise that, liberated from the camps and in attendance at the Council, Slipyj would concelebrate Mass only with fellow cardinals, not with any noncardinal Council Fathers!)

A month later, Adzhubei had his papal audience. Against the advice of some, Genoa's Cardinal Giuseppe Siri encouraged the pope to meet with Adzhubei and his wife on March 7, 1963, three months before the pontiff's death. *Pacem in Terris* was issued the following month.

In 1961 the Soviet Ambassador to Italy gave John XXIII a birthday greeting—the first contact between the Communist state and the Vatican since the Bolshevik Revolution. The Holy Father exploited this opening the following year during the Cuban Missile Crisis, which threatened global annihilation. He therefore begged:

> all governments not to remain deaf to this cry of humanity: that they do all that is in their power to save peace. They will thus spare the world from the horrors of a war whose terrifying consequences no one can predict—that they continue discussions, as this loyal and open behavior has great value as a witness of everyone's conscience and before history. Promoting, favoring, accepting

conversations, at all levels and in any time, is a rule of wisdom and prudence which attracts the blessings of heaven and earth.

Hand-delivered to the U.S. and Soviet embassies, this message was broadcast over Vatican Radio. *Pravda*, the official organ of the Soviet Communist Party, gave it page-one coverage. The pope had been a successful mediator between the superpowers.

Bishop Sheen and I once lunched with Archduke Otto, son of Empress Zita of Bourbon-Parma (Queen of Hungary) and Emperor Charles (Karl) I of Austria.* Sheen was close to the Habsburgs, especially Otto, who often called on Bishop Sheen, seeking advice as well as a blessing. Otto entered Austrian politics, becoming a member of the Austrian Parliament and a member of the European Parliament as well. Sheen had advised him on that too.

Whenever Belgian King Baudouin and Queen Fabiola visited New York, Sheen, the royal family's spiritual director, would invite them to dinner. A saintly couple, they'd decline a security detail that could have found the best route for them when in New York on nonofficial business. Compounded by Manhattan's rush-hour traffic, that decision virtually

---

* Karl is now Blessed, on his way to canonization.

guaranteed a late arrival. As six o'clock approached, we waited for the royals between the doors of our residence's entrance. Deeming me an expert in diplomacy and etiquette, Sheen asked how long we should wait; I suggested 10, 15 minutes. After a quarter hour, it made sense to go inside. Not long after we had descended the stairs for dinner, the doorbell rang, and Frederick, our cook, conducted the king and queen inside. They apologized. It was another incredibly interesting evening.

As the Council took up only three months of the year, most of the time we lived the life of New Yorkers. Bishop Sheen walked the corridors of the city's cultural as well ecclesiastical and political power. In the 1960s, after Vatican II, actress Maureen O'Hara, then in her forties, was a frequent visitor. I also admired the perfect diction of Loretta Young, another Catholic actress. She told us that, almost at the beginning of her career, she was once asked to undress for a scene. "Well," she replied, "you probably have the wrong person," left the soundstage, and went home. Shortly thereafter she was called back. Among his friends the bishop also counted comedians Jackie Gleason, Jack Benny, Henny Youngman, Georgie Jessel, and Milton Berle, many of whom roasted Sheen at the Friar's Club.

In 1967, while I was working at the Apostolic Delegation in Washington, DC, Archbishop (later Cardinal) Egidio Vagnozzi, the nuncio and my superior, called Francesco Colasuonno (later nuncio and cardinal) and me (the kid) into his office. Vagnozzi saw how much work we were doing, but noticed:

"You're typing with two fingers; that's no good!"

So Vagnozzi had us attend the Temple School at night—after working all day!—to learn to type correctly. Dressed in priestly garb, we were the only two guys in a class composed mostly of Black females. The teacher, also an African American, fell in love with us and gave us good marks. Soon I'd be in Rome and that skill would be invaluable, but, frankly, I wouldn't have taken the class had it been up to me.

⸙

Sometime in the mid-sixties (1965 or 1966), Thomas Watson Jr. of IBM would attend Mass at Sheen's residence. One morning after Mass he said:

"At ten o'clock my chauffeur will pick you both up and take you to my office. I have something to show you."

We were driven to IBM's Manhattan headquarters at 590 Madison Avenue—the same address as the 1938 building that was demolished in 1977 to make way for the company's current regional HQ. We were ushered into a huge room populated with immaculately dressed technicians. These wizards proceeded to enthusiastically explain the computer we'd only read about and to show us machines that seemed nearly miraculous in their powers. Turning to me, Watson predicted:

"Father, whatever you see here, and much more, will be one day in your pocket."

The miniaturization of computers we now take for granted confirmed Watson a prophet with honor.

A few months after I arrived in Rome in 1969 a few months after I arrived in Rome to work for the Holy See, I knew the Vatican needed to be brought into the digital age (although we didn't call it that then). My boss was Cardinal Wright, one of five members of the cardinalatial commission that decided such things. Sometime after mentioning my idea, I was invited to speak about computers to the commission. One member, Cardinal Marella, was skeptical. In his Romanesco style, he asked:

"Giovanotto [young man], *how did we get along without this until now?"*

"As a young man yourself, Your Eminence, you were stationed in Washington. I saw your picture. Think of the progress America has made for herself and the whole world in the last 50 years. This is the next step."

Apparently I won the argument, for the Vatican is now probably more computerized than the Italian state.

For New Yorkers, 1966 began in strife as well as celebration. Archbishop Sheen had blessed the inauguration of the handsome, 45-year-old John V. Lindsay on the first day of his first term as New York City's mayor. But the Transit Workers Union struck the Big Apple as soon as its contract expired at 12:01 a.m. New Year's Day. Later that year, former actor Ronald Reagan was elected governor of California. His rousing speech in favor of Barry Goldwater at the 1964 Republican

National Convention put Reagan on the political map; soon he was exploring a run for elected office. Should he? One of the first people whose counsel he sought was (you guessed it) Archbishop Sheen.

⌁⌁⌁

For a couple of weeks in May 1967, I helped Bishop Sheen settle in his residence in his new diocese in Rochester. Then I got a call from Archbishop John Maguire, Coadjutor Archbishop of the Archdiocese of New York.

"Hilary, Rochester is not your diocese. Tomorrow you will get the letter."

Which I did. I was named assistant pastor at Our Lady of Victory (OLV) in Mount Vernon, just north of the Bronx in New York's Westchester County. "That's wonderful!" I thought. "I'm going back to parish work, my first love." There was a lot to do at OLV, so I relished this opportunity. My dream to serve God's people in a parish was about to come true again.

Entrusted to me was, among other things, the Junior Holy Name Society and care of the sick at nearby Mount Vernon Hospital. The Lord blessed us with two vocations during my short stay there: a priest (now a pastor in the archdiocese) and a religious sister (also in parish ministry).

Only five months into this dream assignment, however, I got another call, this time from Monsignor Patrick Ahern, Cardinal Spellman's secretary.

The dream was over.

"Hilary, the Cardinal wants to see you."

Being called to see Cardinal Spellman in those days was usually not for good news. You'd be called only if you or your activities weren't quite right.

"I can't."

"Did you hear what I said?"

"Yes, but unless you want me to leave two corpses in front of the church tomorrow morning, I can't leave. There's no one else to officiate at two funerals. Please tell His Eminence."

After five minutes the phone rang again. It was Monsignor Ahern.

"How about Saturday? Come to the residence."

Saturday arrived, and the railroad took me from Mount Vernon to Grand Central Station, and from there I walked to 452 Madison Avenue; the cardinal's residence connected to Saint Patrick's Cathedral on Fifth Avenue. To my surprise, the cardinal himself opened the door and took my coat. I was relieved to see a smile.

The man who in his youth was the first American to serve in the Roman Curia started talking about Rome. He went on for five or six minutes about the friends he had there. I sat mute.

"You must be wondering why I called you."

"Yes, Your Eminence."

"Well, the Holy Father has named you Secretary of the Apostolic Delegation to the United States, in Washington."

My lack of reaction irritated the cardinal.

"What's the matter with you!? There are 64,000 priests in this country, and you're the first New Yorker to get this appointment. You're not excited?"

"I don't know where the delegation is, Your Eminence; I don't know who the delegate is."

"Come with me."

We climbed the stairs to his room. On his desk was a red phone that had a direct line to the apostolic delegate, the pope's representative in Washington, DC. Picking up the phone, Cardinal Spellman waited for the connection. Archbishop (later Cardinal) Egidio Vagnozzi answered.

"Yes, Your Eminence?"

"Here's Father Franco. He's accepting."

Suddenly I was on the phone with a superior whom I did not know. After some chitchat Vagnozzi asked:

"Do you understand Italian?"

"My mother spoke with me in perfect Italian since my birth, and I got my doctorate in Rome."

"Then, parliamo italiano!" ("Let's speak Italian!")

Cardinal Spellman couldn't follow. It dawned on me: I was now operating at a high level in a new ball game. On the return trip to Mount Vernon I was downcast, for neither did I know what the appointment meant nor could I discuss it. It was *sub secreto*: I had to keep mum until the appointment was published.

I continued parish work for another week or so until, at last, the news broke in the papers. I could now speak freely about the prospects of a life different not only from the parish life I preferred, but also from the work I had done in Rome during the Council.

That's how I was called to our nation's capital. During my years in Washington I lived through events that affected the lives of millions, like the curfew after the assassination of Martin Luther King Jr., the publication of the encyclical *Humanae Vitae*, and the assassination of Bobby Kennedy, to name a few.

One of the things the office of the apostolic delegation to the United Nations dealt with was the nomination of new bishops—about 60 during my time there. In addition, Pope Paul VI created new cardinals, and the Apostolic Delegate was one of the four named in the United States. It fell to me to give him the news, but the delegate wasn't home. He had been at a ceremony in Ohio and didn't return until around 10 that evening. Opening the door, I greeted him, not as "Your Excellency," but rather:

"Your Eminence!"

He was a real *Romano*, with a temper to match. He turned to his driver:

"You see, these youngsters don't even know how to address people properly!"

"Your Eminence!"

"What's the matter with you!?"

"We have received a coded message to be published tomorrow morning. There will be four new cardinals; you're one of them."

Early the following morning I was asked to call the other three: "The apostolic delegate asked me to call you to give you the news."

Archbishop Krol of Philadelphia was one of them, and so was Archbishop Cody of Chicago. The third was my friend Archbishop O'Boyle of Washington, DC. For the first time Washington, DC, would have a cardinal archbishop. Here's how it went with O'Boyle:

"From now on I have to address you as 'Your Eminence.'"

"Come on, Hilary! Is this a joke? We're two kids from the Bronx!"

"No joke! You've been named a Cardinal.... Your Eminence!"

For the two years that I worked in Washington, starting in 1966, the apostolic delegate would regularly assign me tasks that had me traveling to Rome well before my two-dozen-year tour of duty there began. I had a couple of audiences with Pope Paul VI, both administrative in nature. By the time I served as intermediary between Bishop Sheen and the pope, I was already working in Rome.

The Roman Curia's internationalization was the prime mover of my being called to the Eternal City. From 1968 to 1970 I was part of the new Prefecture for Economic Affairs of the Holy See, which audited the budgets and balance sheets of the Vatican's many dicasteries. Cardinal Egidio Vagnozzi, its first president and my recent superior in Washington, had called me in to help.

Sheen wanted to retire from the Diocese of Rochester, and some made a fuss about his retiring before the mandatory age of 75. He wanted his retirement to coincide, not with a milestone birthday, but rather with his completion of 50 years of priestly service, which had begun in 1919. Sheen asked me to convey his wish to the Holy Father. It came true a few months before reaching that more significant milestone in 1969 at the age of 74.

The year 1978 was the "year of three popes," as the title of one book has it. The first of these three pontificates, Paul VI's, was in its fifteenth year. It was marked not only by theological "dissent," but also by terroristic violence that affected the Holy Father deeply and personally. For Giovanni Battista Montini, the kidnapping of Italian Prime Minister Aldo Moro, his friend of 50 years, was both gut-wrenching and heartrending.

The kidnapping shook him to his core. Publicly, he pleaded for Moro's release; privately, he sought to arrange a ransom. It was reported that His Holiness even offered to take Moro's place. Fifty-five days after being kidnapped, however, Moro was executed. On May 13, 1978 (yet *another* May 13th!), Paul VI conducted Moro's funeral at the Basilica of St. John Lateran in Rome. His torment was almost uncontainable:

> And who can listen to our lament, if not you, O God of life and death? You did not hearken to our supplication for the safety of Aldo Moro, this good, meek, wise, innocent and friendly man; but you, O Lord, have not abandoned his immortal spirit, sealed by faith in Christ, who is the Resurrection and the life.

"You did not listen to my prayer"; such words on the lips of a pope shocked not only Italy but the world. I have an original copy of the handwritten letter on which he penned that plea. Even more than four decades later the drama of those days haunts my memory. A broken heart and a seared spirit sapped Pope Paul of his nervous energy. He was dead in less than three months.

Going through memorabilia, which included copies of Pope Paul's handwritten notes, I found a short entry dated December 8, 1965, the Council's closing day. My rough translation: "With the help of God we have concluded the Council today! And now . . . rest? There's no such thing as 'rest' for one who preaches the Gospel!"

After the Council, I served this pope, first in the Vatican's diplomatic corps in Washington (1966 to 1968) and then in the Roman Curia until the day of his death, August 6, 1978. Twenty days later, I witnessed the election of Venerable John Paul I and, a month later, the end of his tragically brief pontificate (August 26, 1978—September 28, 1978).

On May 13, 1966, as I mentioned, I accompanied Bishop Sheen to his audience with Pope Paul VI, who addressed his distinguished guest:

"You've done so much for the Church. We'd like to do something for you. What can we do?"

The pope considered appointing Sheen to head a dicastery in Rome, which could have led to his being created a cardinal. But that would mean relocating to the Vatican and conducting affairs in Italian, rather than his mother tongue. His ministry would be more efficacious, he was convinced, were he to remain closer to home, using the language whose mastery he had demonstrated for a half century in the pulpit, in print, on radio, and on television.

"Your Holiness, I have always obeyed the Vicar of Christ on earth, and so I would abide by whatever you will call me to do, but frankly I would like to have my own people."

The pope understood. Shortly afterward, when I was stationed at the Apostolic Delegation in Washington,* Apostolic Delegate Archbishop (later Cardinal) Egidio Vagnozzi told me the Holy Father had called expressly to ask him to reserve for Bishop Sheen the next worthy available diocese in the United States.

New York State's Diocese of Rochester filled the bill; the retirement of Bishop James Edward Kearney had opened it up. Archbishop Vagnozzi called Sheen's superior, Cardinal Spellman, to inform him of the pope's decision to name Sheen Bishop of Rochester.

Spellman insisted there was no need to promote "his" auxiliary bishop. But, Vagnozzi clarified, getting Spellman's input was not the purpose of the call: he was communicating a directive, not seeking advice.

Misinformation about the relationship between Cardinal Spellman and Bishop Sheen has spread wildly, and this is an opportunity to provide some context.

---

* My work in the nation's capital began in 1967, but the United States didn't have diplomatic relations with the Holy See until 1984. In countries lacking such relations, the pope may send an apostolic delegate to act as a liaison with Rome (but not accredited to their governments). Apostolic delegates have the same rank as nuncios, but no formal diplomatic status. For example, an apostolic delegate served as the Holy See's de facto diplomatic representative to the United States until we established full relations with the Holy See in 1984, allowing for the appointment of a papal nuncio.

In 1925, while serving in the Vatican Secretariat of State (the first American to do so), Monsignor Francis Joseph Spellman struck up a friendship with Eugenio Pacelli, then Cardinal Secretary of State. Six years later, Pope Pius XI tasked Spellman with smuggling the anti-Fascist, anti-Nazi encyclical *Non abbiamo bisogno* out of Rome. It was rumored that Pius intended to replace New York's Cardinal Hayes, who had died in September 1938, with Cincinnati Archbishop John T. McNicholas. He might have carried out that intention had his third heart attack on February 10, 1939, not been fatal. When Cardinal Pacelli was elected pope on March 2nd, he took the title of Pius XII and, six weeks later, named Francis Joseph Spellman, Auxiliary Bishop of Boston since 1932, Archbishop of New York.

There *was* friction between Spellman and Sheen: Spellman wanted to use some funds donated to the Propagation of the Faith for the relief of earthquake victims in the Philippines. America's Military Vicar and Sheen didn't see eye-to-eye on Vietnam (Spellman for American involvement, Sheen against), but we should remember it was Spellman who, in 1951, had named the incredibly popular Fulton J. Sheen as his Auxiliary Bishop of New York.

Six Popes

Pope John XXIII
1958–1963

Pope Paul VI
1963–1978

Pope John Paul I
1978

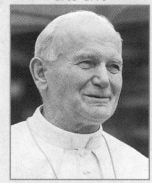

Pope John Paul II
1978–2005

Pope Benedict XVI
2005–2013

Pope Francis
2013–Present

A Son of the Church Remembers

Top: With Saint John XXIII, at the Vatican, circa November 1959.
Middle: With Saint Paul VI and Cardinal John Joseph Wright
(to the left of the Pope), the early 1970s.
Bottom: Around the same years (the early 1970s because
I still have my long sideburns!) with Saint Paul VI.

A Son of the Church Remembers

Top left: A very short time after his election (October 16, 1978),
John Paul II came to visit in my office in Rome.
Top right: With John Paul II in early 1990s (probably 1992) and Cardinal Jose'
Sanchez, and Archbishop (later Cardinal) Crescenzio Sepe.
Bottom: With Saint John Paul II: St. Peter's Square: I am introducing an
American priest from Maryknoll, Father Vincent Mallon, to the Pope (around
1985 because I still have some hair, unruffled by a strong wind).

A Son of the Church Remembers

Top: Concelebrating Mass with John Paul II, in his private chapel
in the Vatican, in the early 1980s. I am holding the red book in my hands
because I would proclaim the Gospel at the Mass.
Bottom: Private audience in the Apostolic Palace in the early 1990s
(I would say in 1993): John Paul II and my Mom, Maria Caterina.

A Son of the Church Remembers

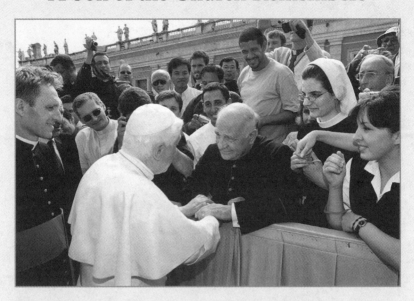

Top: Audience with Pope Benedict XVI in Saint Peter's Square around the year 2008 or 2009. His secretary (who is now an archbishop) is next to the Pope.
Bottom: Concelebrating with Pope Francis at Santa Marta on January 13, 2014 (my name day, Saint Hilary) and this will be repeated several times in the following years on my feast day (name day).

A Son of the Church Remembers

Top: Private audience with Pope Francis in the Private Library of the Pontiff
in the Apostolic Palace, also with Cardinal Peter Kodwo Turkson,
Prefect of the Vatican Dicastery for Promoting Integral Human Development.
Bottom: With Mother Teresa during her last visit to New York. The photo was
taken on June 24, 1997. She will be called by the Lord on September 5, 1997.

A Son of the Church Remembers

Top left: With Rabbi Arthur Schneier, Senior Rabbi
of New York City's Park East Synagogue.
Top right: With Cardinal Terence Cooke, Archbishop of New York,
in the summer of 1980.
Bottom: At the residence (452 Madison Avenue, New York) of Cardinal Francis
Spellman, Archbishop of New York, while the Cardinal is announcing the naming
of the Auxiliary Bishop Fulton J. Sheen (*to his right*) to be the new Bishop of the
Diocese of Rochester, New York. (October 21, 1966) (notice my head . . . full of hair!).

A Son of the Church Remembers

Top left: One of the winters of my 19 years as pastor,
standing in front of Saint Augustine Parish, Ossining, New York.
Top right: My official photo in my office in the Vatican where I had served
for 26 years. The photo was probably taken in 1993.
Bottom: Covering for American television (most likely Fox News)
one of the many important events of the Holy Year 2000.

EIGHT

The Sixties: Upheaval in the World and Church

In caritate perpetua dilexi te,
ideo attraxi te, miserans tui

[I have loved you with an everlasting love,
therefore I have drawn you, taking pity on you]

JEREMIAH 31:3

John F. Kennedy may have been ready to be president years before being elected to that office, but it was Fulton J. Sheen who prepared America culturally for its first Catholic commander in chief.

Before 1928, anti-Catholic prejudice was baked into the American social cake. Protestant propaganda would have one think that if Alfred E. Smith won that year's presidential election, the pope's minions would emerge from the Holland Tunnel and take possession of New York.

Visit Old Saint Patrick's Cathedral on Mulberry Street in Little Italy, and you'll see a brick wall on its Prince Street southern border. The cathedral's defenders built it in the nineteenth century as a bulwark against the anti-Catholic violence of the Know Nothings and other bigoted nativists. By 1928, however, the anti-Catholic tide began to turn.

Bishop Fulton J. Sheen, a pioneer of televised evangelism, was eager to exploit the new medium. After the Second Word War, America needed an inspirational speaker, and he more than qualified. The DuPont Network got him first, and later WABC. He put Catholicism on America's cultural map. Catholicism now had, as we now say, the right "optics."

Kennedy persuaded Catholics that they at least had the *possibility* of electing one of their own as president, even if they didn't agree with everything he said. (The Kennedy family had Boston's Cardinal Richard Cushing for their spiritual director, but as a Catholic, Jack was not exemplary.) Kennedy was a beacon of hope, in large measure due to Sheen's role in accelerating the country's break with its anti-Catholic past.

As I mentioned earlier, there were two occasions in 1963 when I made my way into a church to cry like a baby, the first being the passing of Pope John XXIII on June 3rd. The other was on November 22nd when another John, President Kennedy, was assassinated.

Five years later, I served as master of ceremonies for the apostolic delegate in Saint Patrick's Cathedral for Bobby Kennedy's funeral. Only six months earlier, Bishop Sheen and I had had an impromptu chitchat with Robert Kennedy, New York's junior senator, and his wife, Ethel, at JFK, the airport named in honor of his slain brother. In March Bobby threw his hat into the presidential ring. An assassin's bullet took him from us on June 6th (on which more later).

On February 13, 1969, I was with my boss, Archbishop Luigi Raimondi, apostolic delegate in Washington, when we had dinner at 3339 Massachusetts Avenue (the Apostolic Delegation), with three cardinal archbishops, including John Patrick Cody of Chicago, James Francis McIntyre of Los Angeles, and John Francis Dearden of Detroit. On Leap Day a few weeks later, two things stand out in my memory.

The *New York Times* reported that Sheen had given one of his diocese's churches to the poor. (In November 1964, he had been the only Council Father to speak of "the Church of the Poor.") During his time in Rochester, he never spent one weekend at his residence: he'd go from parish to parish assessing the needs of the people. When he saw an underutilized church, he'd write to the Department of Housing and Urban Development to this effect: "The diocese would like to give this building and land with the provision that you build homes for low-income people." Sheen was the first to do this, and many followed his lead.

But in those days, gifting Church property to the federal government was unheard of. Nearly every bishop was against it. "How dare he do that?!" summed up the consensus.

The same day I read about this, I learned who was to succeed Cardinal Spellman. (He had died the previous December 2nd, just a couple of months before my dinner with Raimondi.) New York had had no archbishop for Advent and Christmas 1967. New York's Coadjutor Archbishop John Joseph Maguire was expected to succeed Spellman, but didn't have the right of succession. The office of the apostolic delegate received a coded message: Terence Cooke, Auxiliary Bishop of New York, was to be named archbishop. Once Cooke was informed, he had to accept the position in person in the apostolic delegate's office. He arrived at four in the afternoon. I went to open the door and said: "Now I can call you archbishop!" He looked a bit surprised. The appointment was announced the following Friday, March 8th.

On March 3rd, Sheen and I had driven to Camden, New Jersey, and stayed overnight at Bishop George Henry Guilfoyle's residence for his installation as Camden's bishop the next day at the Cathedral of the Immaculate Conception. Bishop Guilfoyle had been Director of Catholic Charities in New York as well as Auxiliary Bishop of New York. (Camden is America's poorest diocese.) Among the bishops and prelates present at the installation was John Maguire, Coadjutor Archbishop of New York. This was when Maguire was told of the naming of Bishop Terence Cooke as the new Archbishop of New York.

On the evening of May 7, 1968, at Apostolic Delegate Raimondi's request, I gave Cardinal John Joseph Krol of Philadelphia a courtesy call informing him that Terence Cooke was going to be named New York's archbishop the next day. (Like Cardinal Cody in Chicago, Krol enjoyed a great deal of prestige in the Church in America.) As I knew them all, it would fall to me to communicate similar things to them.

We were enjoying an interval of relative peace before the storm that would descend upon the nation a few weeks later.

The consecration of Bishop Dennis Hickey and Bishop John McCafferty as auxiliary bishops of Sheen's diocese was scheduled for March 14th, and so the day before, I traveled to Rochester with Apostolic Delegate Raimondi, Monsignor D'Arcy, and Father Kelly (a Dominican priest who worked in our Protocol Office). After being picked up at the airport, we had dinner; I stayed at Sheen's residence. The men were consecrated the next morning; there was an official banquet at two in the afternoon; we were on our way back to Washington before six.

On the last day of March, President Johnson announced that he'd neither seek nor accept his party's nomination as its candidate for president. He would not be seeking reelection. A few days later, April 4th, I drove the apostolic delegate to New York for Terence Cooke's installation at Saint Patrick's. A midafternoon banquet in his honor was held three blocks east at the Waldorf Astoria.

At a minute after six that day, Martin Luther King Jr. was assassinated at the Lorraine Motel in Memphis, Tennessee.

On April 6th, Washington, DC, police enforced a four o'clock curfew. I had planned to see Mom in Baltimore the next day, but if I kept that appointment, there was no way I could return by four.

The King funeral in Atlanta, Georgia, was held on April 9th—the thirteenth anniversary of my ordination. There were no official messages from the Vatican for this Baptist minister. There'd be a different response to Bobby Kennedy's murder two months later.

After the celebration of my Easter Mass at Saint Jude's, I went to Baltimore for dinner with Mom and Aunt Rosarina's family. I didn't stay long because Archbishop Raimondi, my boss, was alone at the Apostolic Delegation on this festive day. When I was back at the Delegation, the archbishop recalled the time when he was secretary to Cardinal Amleto Giovanni

Cicognani.* As Raimondi had done for his superior, it was my turn to play dominoes with Raimondi. This game was new to me, but I'm a quick learner.

A few days later, April 19th, I had dinner with Raimondi and a guest named Carlos from Mexico. Raimondi, recently nuncio to that country, was connected to Mexico's most powerful families.

A week later, April 26th, a Friday, a reception for King Olaf V of Norway was held at the Norweigan Embassy which was located next door to the Apostolic Delegation. In my presence President Lyndon Johnson privately inquired of the nuncio if Pope Paul would be willing to host peace talks for the end of the Vietnam War. We hurried back to the office to teletype Rome, not expecting a reply until the next day. The immediate affirmative reply from the Holy Father excited us. He was more than willing to host those talks in the Vatican's Apostolic Palace. To this day I cherish a copy of President Johnson's letter of gratitude to the pope. Of course, the Communist Viet Cong had zero interest in accepting this offer.

On April 29, 1968, Archbishop Raimondi received a request from the Vatican that I be called to a post there. I'd remain in Washington for two more months. They wouldn't be quiet months. As I already mentioned, Senator Robert Kennedy, whose path Archbishop Sheen and I had crossed only a few months earlier, was assassinated on June 6th. Raimondi, my boss, asked me to prepare a message of condolences for Ethel,

---

* Cicognani was then apostolic delegate (1933–1958), later Vatican Secretary of State (1961–1969) and Dean of the College of Cardinals. Before all that, he had spent 26 years as the apostolic delegate of the Holy See in Washington, from the beginning of FDR's presidency in 1933 until the end of Eisenhower's in 1959.

his widow. I made bold to suggest that such a message would not be enough. Given the present situation the Delegate himself should be present at the funeral.

"We only attend the funerals of presidents."

"But Bobby Kennedy counts for more than five presidents. We have to do more," I gently pushed back. I was ready to prepare the telegram for the widow when we received a coded message: Pope Paul VI had named Cardinal Angelo Dell'Acqua as his personal legate to the funeral. The nuncio's attitude quickly conformed to the new reality. He asked me to leave for New York to meet Dell'Acqua at JFK Airport. The nuncio arrived the following day to attend the funeral.

I went to John F. Kennedy Airport to receive Dell'Acqua. Lee Radziwill, Jacqueline Bouvier Kennedy's sister, had deplaned on the tarmac not far from me. Smiling, his natural disposition, the cardinal descended the aircraft's stairs. (No passenger boarding bridges in those days.)

"Your Eminence, this is a funeral."

He adjusted his countenance.

Since 1964 the Vatican has had a Permanent Observer to the United Nations. The first one, Monsignor Alberto Giovanetti, was in the greeting party. Visibly agitated, he approached me.

"You have to save the situation!"

The visit of the pope's personal legate was news. A gaggle of reporters gathered to await Cardinal Dell'Acqua's arrival.

Stepping up to the microphones, Dell'Acqua began delivering the statement he apparently cobbled together on the plane—in Italian! I was pressed into the service of impromptu translator, maybe because I had translating experience—or because I was the only one around with a command of both Italian and English! I translated not only the Cardinal's statement, but also reporters' questions into Italian and his answers.

That Saturday, June 8th (coincidentally, the day James Earl Ray was arrested in London for the murder of Martin Luther King), a High Requiem Mass for Bobby Kennedy was concelebrated at Saint Patrick's Cathedral. President Johnson, Lady Bird Johnson, and several cabinet members were in attendance. Also present was Richard Cardinal Cushing of Boston, the Kennedy family's spiritual director. The president graciously arranged for Air Force One to return Cushing, who was visibly ill, to Boston after Kennedy's body arrived in Washington by train with the presidential party. (Cushing could not attend the burial at Arlington National Cemetery.) Being a friend of Cushing's, I called him around seven the next morning to ask about his health.

"Young man, did you say Mass yet?"

"No, Your Eminence."

"Well, I did, and I'm just fine!"

That captures the great churchman I remember: always on-the-go, exuding boundless energy sweetened by a sense of humor. Before my departure for Rome a week later, I visited him for the last time, and lunched with another friend, John Cardinal Krol.

By July 16, 1968, my 36th birthday, I was settled in the Eternal City. A car is a must-have when working in Rome and living at Villa Stritch (about which more later) and driving to and from my Vatican office. Getting a car took time, but eventually I settled on a new Alfa Romeo Giulia Super. It cost only $2,352 (approximately $17,483 today, about what you'd pay to add this vintage car to your collection now). I bought it with Italian lira, of course, and since the exchange rate was 625 lira to the U.S. dollar, the price tag was 1.4 million Italian lira. So, you could say I drove a millionaire's car. My office was now only seven minutes away.

I didn't then understand why my monthly salary in Washington was $119. Why not $120? When I got to Rome, I learned the secret that since we were part of the Vatican establishment, the apostolic delegate in Washington paid us in lira, which equated to 119 U.S. dollars. Vatican precision at its finest!

Villa Stritch is the residence for American priests working in the Vatican. Pope Saint Paul VI blessed it on June 29, 1968. One of its 13 original residents, I lived there for 26 years. A fruit of the internationalization of the Roman Curia, a Vatican II goal, it was provided for us by the United States Conference of Catholic Bishops.

When on official visits to the Vatican, members of the American hierarchy would be guests. We'd also invite officials of the Roman Curia to break bread with us. On November 13, 1968, for example, we lunched with Cardinals Alfredo Ottaviani (Pro-Prefect of the Congregation for the Doctrine of the Faith)* and Paolo Marella (president of the then-new dicastery for Non-Christians). On Thanksgiving that year our guests included the following cardinals, among other dignitaries: Amleto Giovanni Cicognani (Secretary of State), Angelo Dell'Acqua (Vicar of the Holy Father for the Diocese of Rome), and John Krol (Archbishop of Philadelphia).

A future superior of mine, Cardinal Edward Egan (1932– 2015), Archbishop of New York, was a fellow Villa Stritch resident for 14 of my 26 years there. In 1971 Pope Saint Paul VI named him, then a monsignor, auditor of the Sacred Roman Rota. When he became a consultor for my work in the Congregation for the Clergy (about which more later), he was already a friend.

On November 15th, I registered to enroll in a two-year course of study at the Pontifical Lateran University in the faculty called *utroque*, that is, civil law and canon law. Vatican workers-students were dispensed from having to attend classes at the university, which meant I could study at home. Later that day I met with Monsignor Pio Laghi, the man who had introduced Bishop Sheen and me to Mother Teresa. Laghi was named apostolic delegate to Jerusalem and Palestine the following May and consecrated bishop the month after that.

November continued to be busy: John Cardinal Kroll visited me on the 25th; Kroll, Angelo Cardinal Dell'Acqua, and Amleto Cardinal Giovanni Cicognani celebrated Thanksgiving with us at Villa Stritch on the 28th.

---

* Formerly called Sant'Uffizio, the Holy Office.

NINE

Working in the Vatican

Every moment of life is like a sacrament
in which we can receive God.
It is a channel through which God speaks to us,
forms us, and directs us.

MOTHER ANGELICA

In 1969, Paul VI did something unusual: he created a diocesan bishop a cardinal and then immediately appointed him head of a dicastery. The man was John Joseph Wright, Bishop of Pittsburgh. As cardinal he was named Prefect of the Congregation for the Clergy. Cardinal Wright would be my boss for 10 years when I was named an official of that dicastery.

During the two years I worked in Washington, the apostolic delegate* would regularly send me to Rome. As I mentioned earlier, I had had a couple of administrative audiences with Pope Paul VI. When I served as the intermediary between Bishop Sheen and the pope, I was already working in Rome. During my years at the Apostolic Delegation, I often wondered whether Rome really knew what was going on with

---

* Now the apostolic nuncio. The Holy See and the United States didn't have full diplomatic relations until 1984.

American Catholics. Being far from the scene, perhaps Rome took measures that didn't reflect reality.

But then I got to Rome, which has a macrocosmic view of the world's problems, a global horizon, a universal approach, not a limited, microcosmic perspective. The Vatican has in view the needs of all countries, not only the United States of America and Great Britain, but also Bangladesh and East Timor. The Church's growth in Africa *and* decline in Europe are of equal concern. So is Asia. Rome expanded my horizons. Being there forced me to look at things globally.

After the Council, the internationalization of the Roman Curia grew in importance. The dicastery I was called to in 1970 had been known as the Congregation of the Council (*Sacra Congregatio Concilii*) since the days of the Council of Trent (1545–1563), but now it's the Congregation for the Clergy. When I arrived, nearly all its officials were Piedmontese—not just Italian, but Piedmontese!—and they were nearing retirement. Yet as soon as he was created a cardinal, John Joseph Wright, formerly Bishop of Pittsburgh, was called to head this dicastery. After the Council, the English-speaking world woke up, so to speak, and we began to receive many letters that made requests of every kind.

There was no clergy shortage in 1970. That year our dicastery convened a Congress in Malta to discuss the Distribution of the Clergy. When I was ordained in 1955, ours was a class of more than 40 ordinands. You couldn't realistically expect to be named a pastor of a parish until you were at least 65. Due to an abundance of vocations and ordained priests, the issue was debated at length at Malta. Later on, the Congregation of the Clergy decided that a pastor's term limit would be six years, renewable depending upon the local bishop's decision and the diocese's needs. The 1983 Code of Canon Law codified this. Canon 522 states: "A pastor must possess stability and therefore is to be appointed for an indefinite period of time. The diocesan bishop can appoint him only for a specific period if the conference of bishops has permitted this by a decree." Sometimes the local bishop would misinterpret (or misapply) this canon, and our Congregation for the Clergy would handle "recourses" that affected pastors would submit to our office.

Our dicastery had three spheres of responsibility. One such office covered the discipline of the clergy and the needs of the bishops. The second was catechetical, which reviewed catechisms and other texts for religious education for their orthodoxy; and the third concerned finances, a spectrum of competencies. Any diocese whose operation exceeded a million dollars needed to clear that magnitude with the Vatican. (During my time, we increased the limit from $1 million to $3 million.)

Still a young official of this dicastery, I had the English-speaking world as my oyster. When I got there, I asked

Monsignor Baudas, a Hungarian native and my predecessor, if he had advice for this kid. I inquired (in Italian):

"I'm sure you speak English . . . ?"

A world-weary sigh of resignation escaped his lips:

"*Giovanotto* [young man], *my only language is my mother tongue, Hungarian. I have some Latin, and now some Italian. That's it. Why do I need English?*"

"Well, this discastery is also supposed to serve the English-speaking world, no?"

"*Yes, but all you have to do . . .*"

He handed me a "rescript," a form on which one requests permission to do or receive something in the requester's diocese. All in Latin.

"*. . . What's the name of your diocese?*"

"New York."

"*So, you write 'Dioecesis Neo-Eboracensis.' Then you mail it.*"

I tried again:

"Surely you visited some English-speaking countries and picked up something of their cultures?"

"*Giovanotto, since leaving Hungary after the 1956 revolution, I haven't ventured much beyond Rome . . . maybe Frascati and some Castelli Romani.*"

Those Roman castles were less than an hour's drive from us. Monsignor Baudas may have handled requests from English-speaking countries, but there was no "English Desk" to speak of. Another official took care of Francophones, another Hispanophones, and so on. But most of those "officials" were Italians. Even to have a Hungarian was highly unusual. Monsignor Baudas was off to his next adventure, the Vatican's Secretariat of State.

Even when I opposed the direction taken by a superior, I'd carry out his directives. But one time I made an exception.

My dicastery's prefect had accepted the invitation of an organization of conservative activist American Catholics, which shall remain nameless, to address their inaugural meeting. The Cardinal Prefect directed me to ready a letter of acceptance for him to sign, but without first informing the American bishops' governing body.

I noticed the organization's name. It was a sketchy, somewhat controversial outfit.

"You're not going."

"Whoa! What do you mean, I'm not going? Just write the letter and give it to me to sign!"

"No, you're not accepting. They're not balanced. Your appearance would cause problems."

"But I want to go!"

"I'll arrange something else, if you'd like, but, please, don't go to that meeting."

I left his office. He delegated the acceptance letter–writing to someone outside of our office.

He attended the event, and predictably, a public relations disaster followed. His brothers in the American episcopate learned that the Prefect of the Congregation for the Clergy had attended the meeting of that group. They were not amused. That's the long and short story of the episode of my "insubordination."

༄༅༄

One day we got a letter from Mother Mary Angelica, the Poor Clare foundress of Eternal Word Television Network (EWTN), then America's only nationwide Catholic cable channel. The many obstacles local bishops had placed in her way brought EWTN to the verge of collapse. You see, they had their own local television channels in their dioceses, and neither needed nor wanted competition from other Catholics.

Mother Angelica pleaded with us to ask the Conference of American Catholic Bishops to support her groundbreaking ministry. If the Vatican won't go to bat for EWTN, she feared, she'd have to shutter it. I composed for the prefect's signature a letter outlining why American bishops should support her ministry.

Apparently, it did the trick. As I write, EWTN is still doing a tremendous job promoting the Faith in the United States and around the world. More than 100 million American homes carry this channel. I'm gratified to have played any small part in this reversal of misfortune.

༄༅༄

As I have already mentioned, the work at the third office of the Congregation for the Clergy was related to the Church's day-to-day operations both in the Vatican and dioceses around the world.

Fiscal reality rarely corresponds to the ideal, and that mismatch can make "bosses" look like bad guys. Monsignor

Edward Egan (later Cardinal Archbishop of New York) and Monsignor Cormac Murphy-O'Connor (later Cardinal Archbishop of Westminster) were two consultors for my work at the Congregation for the Clergy. We made tough decisions in the face of changing demographics in a changing world.

By contrast, one parish had what one might call a "high-class problem": Saint Augustine by-the-Sea on Waikiki Beach, Honolulu, Hawaii. No amount of money offered could persuade the parish to sell.

Bishop Joseph Ferrario of Honolulu entered my office. As I said, one of the competencies of the Congregation for the Clergy was the handling of financial problems of this kind. And so this one, arising from a prospective sale, landed on my desk.

"Japanese investors have approached me with an offer of $7 million for the church property on Waikiki Beach. Here's the documentation and my acceptance letter."

"Leave everything here," I said. "I'll look into it."

Soon delegations from Honolulu came to me with their insistent rejection of any offer. To them, their church was, historically and spiritually, of inestimable value. You see, Saint Augustine's is where the ministry of Father (later Saint) Damien of Molokai began.

The next offer was $12 million.

The third or fourth, $27 million.

To Honolulu we dispatched our consultant, Virgil C. Dechant, then Supreme Knight of the Knights of Columbus, to investigate. His report's bottom line? The site's significance was such that we couldn't touch it. Soon Bishop Ferrario was back in my office, both irritated and puzzled that he hadn't gotten our permission to sell for a king's ransom.

I motioned the bishop to my big window. Opening onto the Piazza San Pietro, it had a view of Bernini's semicircular marble colonnade that embraces, as though with two arms, visitors to Saint Peter's Square.

"Tomorrow I'm going to sell one of those columns," I said. "That should take care of the Vatican's budget deficit."

"*What!?*"

"Well, how's that different from what you're proposing to do for $27 million? You'd be depriving not only Saint Augustine's parishioners, not only Honoluluans, but Catholics the world over, present and to come, of a piece of their Catholic heritage."

Unlike many of New York's parishes that have been on the brink of being closed, Saint Augustine by-the-Sea was populous, active, and financially self-sufficient.

Not amused, Bishop Ferrario stormed out of my office.

Many years later, while pastor of *another* Saint Augustine's in New York's Westchester County, I received a gigantic "Thank You" Christmas card signed by the people of Saint Augustine's. The Fathers of the Congregation of the Sacred Hearts of Jesus and Mary, St. Damien's missionary institute, also expressed their gratitude.

Things went the other way in the Diocese of Rochester, New York. Without asking the Vatican's permission, the diocese decided to sell the once-prestigious Saint Bernard's Seminary to Eastman Kodak for an amount Bishop Matthew Clark couldn't pass up. Later, Kodak sold this complex of buildings to a developer who converted the complex into a senior living facility. Ironically, Kodak itself survived bankruptcy in 2012 only by shedding most of the operations that had made it famous for over a century.

❧

A parish that once flourished, but can no longer sustain its past success, must either "downsize," which might require it to combine its resources with those of nearby parishes, or, sadly, sell some or all of its buildings. I know whereof I speak.

As you recall, my first assignment was to Our Lady of Mount Carmel in the Bronx. Sixty-two thousand people, overwhelmingly Italian-Americans, filled our pews weekly! There are few, if any, remnants of that Italian foundation. I doubt OLMC's regular parishioners today exceed a thousand. Will there be a turnaround? No one can predict future gentrification, but it's unlikely. Rome once ended at the walls of the Archbasilica of St. John Lateran. Now almost half the city is outside those walls.

TEN

John Paul II: Council Father, Cardinal, Pope, Saint

There is no limit to the amount of good you can do,
if you don't care who gets the credit.

RONALD REAGAN

⌦⌧

I'm glad the radio in my Alfa Romeo Giulia Super was on as I was speeding from the Vatican to Villa Stritch on October 16, 1978. I hadn't gone far before the announcer reported that *fumata bianca*, white smoke, was billowing from a stove inside the Sistine Chapel, signaling the election of a new pope.

Executing a sharp U-turn, I reversed course and joined the burgeoning crowds in Saint Peter's Square in under 10 minutes. Awaiting the announcement, I recognized someone on the balcony: Cardinal Pericle Felici—my fellow alumnus and the Vatican Council's General Secretary:

"Habemus Papam!" ("We have a Pope!")

"Eminentissimum et Reverendissimus Dominum Carolum Cardinalem . . ." ("The most Eminent and Reverend Carol Cardinal . . .")

Carol?!

The world expected the centuries-old tradition to hold and an Italian to be elected. Among Italian cardinals, however, there was only one "Carolus" (Charles): Carlo Confalonieri, Dean of the College of Cardinals—and he was 85 years old!

"This can't be," I thought for a split-second before Felici's next word relieved the suspense:

"... *Wojtyla!*"

The world heard the magical, decidedly non-Italian name of Karol Wojtyła—the once-young Auxiliary Bishop of Krakow, then Cardinal Archbishop of Krakow, my friend from the days of the Council!

So, it could be true, after all, and so it was! I would serve him as my pontiff for the next 27 years, that is, until he departed this world on April 2, 2005. Shortly before that fateful day, he arranged to have a parchment blessing, inked in calligraphy, in time for the Golden Jubilee of my priestly ordination on April 9, 2005. One result of engaging the calligraphers in advance, however, was that the parchment eerily bears the date he didn't live to see. Some would call this a "collector's item," a document signed by the pope on April 9th—seven days *postmortem*!

As important to me as the anniversary was, I couldn't bear to miss my friend's funeral, even if that meant hurriedly booking flights for a three-day trip. Then–New York Senator Alfonse D'Amato accompanied me on this whirlwind trip.* The funeral being that Friday, D'Amato and I flew to Rome on Wednesday, April 6th. On Thursday we paid our respect to the pope's exposed body. Four million people lined up to get a last glimpse, so I'm grateful we were able to use a special entrance. The solemn funeral for my friend, attended by heads

---

* Al D'Amato had been a good friend since being elected to the U.S. Senate in November 1980. A few weeks later, President Jimmy Carter sent him to Italy as his emissary, bringing relief to the victims of the Irpinia earthquake, whose epicenter was in Conza di Campania. I received him upon his arrival in Rome and stayed with him throughout his visit. Our friendship grew, and in 1994 he attended my installation as pastor of Saint Augustine in Ossining, New York.

of state the world over and tens of thousands of the faithful, filled Saint Peter's Square. I took it all in, processing both the spiritual and personal loss of his death, yet mindful of the logistical challenges I faced immediately after.

We departed Rome early Saturday, arriving in Newark at 2:30 p.m. Senator D'Amato's connections made it possible for us to be driven directly to Ossining, where we arrived at 4:15. Now safely back at Saint Augustine's (already filled to capacity), I had barely enough time to freshen up and meet my brother concelebrants at the altar by 5:00: Archbishop Celestino Migliore, the Apostolic Nuncio and Permanent Observer of the Holy See to the United Nations, Archbishop Gabriel Montalvo Higuera, Apostolic Nuncio to the United States, who had traveled from the nation's capital for the occasion, and many other priest friends. The priesthood of Jesus Christ, which we shared, was our liturgy's focus, in a special way for me, now having been a priest for half a century. At its conclusion, we all repaired to the school's gymnasium for a grand reception. Around 8:00 or 8:30, my circle of archbishops, priests, authorities, and many other invited guests, including the senator, prolonged the celebration at the Crowne Plaza Hotel in White Plains for an official dinner.

No one can deny the role John Paul II played in the collapse of the Soviet empire, and therefore in ending the Cold War and its attendant four decades of nuclear terror. In this regard Paul Kengor wrote about the joint efforts of John Paul II and President Ronald Reagan:

Philosophically, the two leaders shared an understanding of the reinforcing relationship of faith and freedom, the importance of ordered liberty, and the evil of atheistic, totalitarian communism. They seemed to sense this philosophical kinship before they ever met; they began a rich correspondence in the first year of Reagan's presidency that set the tone for their later meetings. Reagan recognized the importance of a partnership with the pope even before he became president: footage of the pope's 1979 trip to Poland moved him to tears and convinced him that John Paul II "would help change the world." The pope was "the key," and Reagan was intent on making him and the Vatican an ally.[*]

Working in the Vatican at the time, I remember President Reagan's one-day visit to the pope at the height of the negotiations that culminated in the Berlin Wall's razing in 1989. It wasn't a state visit to Italy, but Italian President Sandro Pertini seized the opportunity to invite President Reagan and First Lady Nancy to lunch at the Quirinale Palace.

Pope John Paul II inaugurated efforts "to change the world" during his pontificate's first year, which included a historic first trip to Poland in 1979 and continued with his not-so-secret support of Lech Wałęsa and the movement he led, Solidarność (Solidarity). Tad Szulc, the late *New York Times* journalist, wrote about these events in his biography, *Pope John Paul II.* I came in for a mention:

---

[*] Paul Kengor, *The Pope and the President: John Paul II, Ronald Reagan, and the Extraordinary Untold Story of the 20th Century* (Intercollegiate Studies Institute, 2017), 538.

Late in August [1980], John Paul II wrote a private letter to [Soviet Communist Party General Secretary Leonid] Brezhnev, the first of at least two such missives, assuring him that the unrest in Poland was no threat to the Soviet Union. The letter was hand-carried to Moscow by Monsignor Hilary C. Franco, an American who is a senior official of the Congregation for the Clergy, as were other items of secret correspondence between the Vatican and the Soviets. Monsignor Franco will not specifically confirm that he had carried letters from the pope to Brezhnev and that on each occasion he had to wait a number of days for replies, but he acknowledges being in Moscow in August 1980, "jogging along the Kremlin" to while away the time.*

It is important to note that when Szulc asked to interview me about John Paul II, I accepted because I was told he had interviewed other Vatican officials for this project. I couldn't, however, imagine that he'd ask the kind of questions I wasn't qualified to answer, such as the one quoted in the excerpt. I insisted he not write anything that went beyond his original request. If Tad was looking for a "scoop," he was not going to get one from me.

May 13th has come up several times. That date in 1981, however, is seared into my memory. It fell on a Wednesday, just

---

* Tad Szulc, *Pope John Paul II* (Simon & Schuster, 1995), 373.

another workday for me. The Roman sun lit up my office in the late afternoon, making it oppressively hot. I swung the tall windows open. Thousands were waving to John Paul II as the popemobile ferried him around Saint Peter's Square, generating the unique sonic atmosphere of crowds.

About twenty minutes after five, the joy was shattered.

Crack-crack-crack-crack.

A collective shout went up, followed by eerie silence. Thousands gulped air and held their breath. I ran to the window: John Paul II had been shot four times, wounded seriously, and rushed to the hospital.

Time stood still for millions around the world, but especially for those of us who worked in the Vatican. Prayerfully, we awaited diagnosis and prognosis. What remains with me is not speculation about who put Ali Ağca in Saint Peter's Square or the gun in his hand. Rather, it is the Christ-emulating love of one's enemies, the virtue demonstrated by the Holy Father when he forgave Ağca in his prison cell.

The significance of May 13th was not lost on His Holiness: the anniversary of the Virgin Mary's first apparition to the children at Fátima in 1917. He believed the attempt on his life accorded with the third of three prophecies or "secrets" that Mary had entrusted to them. He firmly believed she saved his life that day. A year later he donated a bullet recovered from the popemobile to Fátima's local bishop. And the bishop had it set in the crown of the statue of Mary in the shrine of Fátima.

There are details I could comment on. For example, the ambulance's siren and horn were out of order that afternoon. But rivers of ink have been wasted on such minutiae; I won't add another tributary.

According to Tad Szulc, the CIA assessed Moscow's view of an attempt on the pope's life this way: his role as aggravator of Moscow's Polish troubles was outweighed by his moderating influence. I earned another mention in Szulc's biography:

> John Paul II's private contacts with the Soviets since the December 1980 visit to him by Vadim Zagladin, the high official of the Soviet Communist Party's Central Committee, and the letters between the Vatican and Moscow secretly carried by Monsignor Hilary Franco early in 1981, had indeed given the Kremlin the sense that he was striving for moderate evolution—and not confrontation—in Poland.*

Sheen's handwritten letters to me before the conclave that culminated in Saint John Paul II's election to the papacy (October 16, 1978) show he had foreseen what the new pope would be and do, including with respect to the fall of the Soviet empire.

---

* Tad Szulc, *Pope John Paul II* (Simon & Schuster, 1995), 393. In 1982 I helped Marvin Kalb prepare and participated in the recording of "The Man Who Shot the Pope: A Study in Terrorism," his *NBC White Paper* televised documentary. I have another reason to recall this in gratitude: while taping on July 16th, Kalb surprised me with a dinner and birthday gift.

ELEVEN

Back in New York: From Ossining to Turtle Bay

*Too often we participate in
the globalization of indifference.
May we strive instead
to live global solidarity.*

POPE FRANCIS

Inot only worked in the Vatican for 26 years (1968–1994), but was also blessed with (at least) *another* 26 years of service to Christ's Church, no less filled with challenges and surprises than the preceding two decades-plus. Here's how God closed one door and opened another in 1994.

Many parishes (in addition to the one in Honolulu discussed earlier) honor Saint Augustine, and one of them lay in my future. Founded in 1853, it's in Ossining, New York. That city has another parish, named after Saint Ann. It was founded in 1927 when Ossining's Italian-Americans had increased their presence. Not welcomed at Saint Augustine's, they formed their own parish and built their own church. It remained solidly Italian for about 60 years. It still celebrates Italian feasts, but probably no more than a hundred of the founding Italian families remain. Their kids don't speak Italian. Tagalog-speaking Filipinos rub shoulders with Hispanophone Ecuadorians.

They continue the migrant's story that evokes Abram, the "pagan" whom God called to be the father of many nations and renamed Abraham.* But even though in 1994 Saint Ann's was still considered an Italian parish, it was not the parish that would one day be entrusted to me. Here's how I got the Saint Augustine's assignment.

When ordained in 1955, I had one purpose: to serve the people as a parish priest. I thanked God for my summer appointments as well as for the time to assist Bishop Sheen to prepare for the Council. By 1994, however, I yearned for parish life. I raised this with Cardinal John Joseph O'Connor, my archbishop.

I had first met O'Connor when he was stationed in New York as Auxiliary Bishop of the Archdiocese for the Military Services, USA.† He had been bishop of Scranton, Pennsylvania, for a year before being named, in 1984, Archbishop of New York. Pope John Paul II created him cardinal the following year. Then serving in the Vatican, I had the privilege of witnessing the pope's imposition of the *biretta* on the head of my new archbishop. O'Connor and I got along very well. My dicastery (the "English Desk") afforded us many occasions to address New York's issues. He phoned me while I was in Rome, asking

---

* Had Abram momentarily thought, "Which god?," the answer he probably got, directly or indirectly, was, "I'm the *only* one, and I'm telling you to leave Ur." "But I'm comfortable here! I'm doing all right!" "You'll go, and I'll tell you where to. You won't be 'Abram' anymore, but rather *Abraham*, the father of many nations." At God's word, Abraham migrated from Ur to Canaan, the promised land. To do that he needed faith, which was accredited to his spiritual account as righteousness (Galatians 3:6).

† It had been the Military Ordinariate of the Archdiocese for the Military Services of the United States before Pope John Paul II reorganized it as an archdiocese in 1986 with its own archbishop. Its see is based in the District of Columbia.

about my mother's health, expressing his condolences when my brother passed away at the relatively young age of 57. And so, after 26 years of service for the Holy See, I put before him my request to return to New York to serve the people of God in my diocese.

Request granted!

He asked me to choose from among several then-open parishes, at first suggesting one in Manhattan's Financial District.

"It's plush. You'll like it. You deserve it."

Over the next two weekends I looked it over. Catholics *did* flock to it—but only during the week! It's in the Financial District; virtually nothing was happening on weekends. I wanted to be active, and made this plain to my superior. O'Connor soon phoned me.

"The pastor at Saint Augustine's in Ossining wants to retire a year earlier. Visit it; see if you like it. It's where I want to retire when my work's done. They have an extra apartment."

Thirty-five acres facing the Hudson. The rectory was far from the church. But what did I know?

"I'll take it."

"Don't you want to see it first? The school has over 200 children."

"If that's where *you* intend to retire, it'll be more than all right for me."

By the time I left Saint Augustine's in 2013, the Holy Spirit had given that parish six vocations: two priests and four permanent deacons. We had built an addition to the school, which now educates over 600 students. In 1997 our "meditation garden," landscaped upon what was once an ugly slope, was enlivened by Stations of the Cross *al fresco*, designed and sculpted by Nino Di Simone from Castelli in the Abbruzzo region of Italy. He and his two sons arrived from Italy to direct the Cartalemi family's dozens of artisans to set the stations in 15 outdoor temples, which were built in six weeks in the style of the main church. Along with two works by Henri Matisse (stained glass and a rose window in Sleepy Hollow), these stations have been declared one of the 10 artistic pearls of Westchester County. Cardinal O'Connor blessed these treasures and consecrated the church's new marble main altar on the evening of March 24, 1997. He was impressed with how much the parish had accomplished in such a short time. (He had just deplaned at JFK, back from Rome, but instead of stopping off at his Manhattan residence, he headed straight to Saint Augustine's.) Sadly, however, O'Connor didn't live to enjoy his planned retirement. He went to be with the Lord on May 3, 2000. He had given this son of Italian immigrants the opportunity to pastor a parish that once didn't welcome them. For occasioning that irony I will always be grateful to him.

The loss of Cardinal O'Connor was offset by the naming of my good friend Edward Egan to succeed him as Archbishop of New York. As mentioned earlier, I knew him as a fellow resident of Villa Stritch for 14 of my 26 years in Rome. In those days he was Monsignor Egan, a judge of the Roman Rota and consultor for my dicastery, the Congregation for the Clergy for cases that arose in the Anglophone world. In the early months of his term as New York's archbishop, he'd refer to me in gatherings of clergy and friends as someone "for whom I used to work while I was in Rome."*

Our friendship deepened during his New York tenure. We met as often as his schedule allowed at a downtown restaurant to chat and reminisce about our Roman days over a dish of spaghetti. I remember his confiding in me about the then-sorry state of the archdiocese's finances. He righted that boat splendidly before his mandatory retirement in 2009.

One Sunday (as I had done several times before at his invitation) I took the railroad from Westchester to meet him in New York City. Arriving at Grand Central, I emerged into the daylight from that terminal's 47th Street exit, the closest to the Cardinal's Madison Avenue residence behind Saint Pat's. I rang the bell. Being the only one there that day, he greeted me at the outer door. He forgot, however, that the inner door locks when shut. So, here we were on the few steps between the two doors, locked out.

Of course, Cardinal Egan hadn't taken his keys. I offered to go next door to the rectory of Saint Patrick's Cathedral, in the hope of finding a duplicate key.

"I'll come with you."

Dressed casually, he startled the secretary who, of course, had no idea where the necessary key was. I tested nearly every key found in the security guard's desk (the guard, of course, was not around) until I found the right one.

Unlike his predecessor, Cardinal Egan enjoyed six years of mandatory retirement before the Lord called him on March 5, 2015. Father Douglas Crawford, his private secretary (who for

---

* Installed as archbishop on June 19, 2000, Egan was created cardinal by Pope John Paul II on February 21, 2001.

the first two years after ordination had served as my associate at Saint Augustine's) relayed the sad news.

Egan's successor, Timothy Michael Dolan, was named Archbishop of New York in 2009. Early in his administration I invited him to a gala dinner at Saint Augustine's to accept our Man of the Year award. Before the dinner he had celebrated Mass, and from the altar he told the congregation one reason he had accepted the invitation: when he was studying theology at the North American College, he used to visit me in my Vatican office. Our friendship grew and has continued since my resignation from Saint Augustine's in July 2013 (after 19 years). Exactly one year later, Cardinal Dolan contributed a beautiful foreword to my book *Bishop Sheen: Mentor and Friend*.*

The year 2000 was a Holy Year, but also a Grand Jubilee Year. Pope John Paul II tasked the Congregation for the Clergy, with which I was consulting, with organizing meetings for priests and bishops on five continents. For Africa, we chose Yamoussoukro, Ivory Coast; for Asia, Jerusalem; for the Americas, Guadalupe; for Europe, Fátima; the final meeting in 2000 convened in Rome.

In Guadalupe, we made history. At the end of the twentieth century the anticlerical laws of the 1917 Mexican Constitution, enforced rigorously by President Plutarco Calles (1877–1945), were still on the books. Those laws prohibited priests from wearing clerical attire, including collars. Yet wear them we did,

---

* Timothy Michael Cardinal Dolan, "Foreword," in Hilary C. Franco, *Bishop Fulton J. Sheen: Mentor and Friend* (New Hope Publications, 2014), xiii–xiv.

and in public! Furthermore, the Constitution forbade processions outside a church, but all of us—more than 2,000 bishops and priests with many of the faithful—processed outside the shrine of Our Lady of Guadalupe. This hadn't happened since before the anti-Christian revolution of 1917 and its persecution of the Cristeros in the 1920s. We challenged those unjust statutes, not with words, but with actions.

As I write this, Donald J. Trump is now former president of the United States. Before his election in 2016, I had met him several times at his National Golf Club in Briarcliff Manor, less than 10 minutes from Saint Augustine's.

I'm no golfer, but Louis Rinaldi is. Hailing from Uruguay, Lou is a successful entrepreneur, running his own construction business. When I first met Trump, he was already a phenomenally successful businessman and star of the hit TV show *The Apprentice*. Both Lou and Donald Trump became friends and golf buddies.

I caught a glimpse of Trump's personal side in 2012 when Lou's son Robert was diagnosed with cancer. When Trump got that terrible news, he began to spend more time with Lou and Robert. During this difficult time the billionaire's upbeat disposition kept up Robert's spirits. He even arranged for Robert to get the best treatment, wherever in the world it could be gotten. When hope for remission ran out, Robert and his fiancé Courtney went ahead with their wedding plans. I blessed their wedding, which, of course, Trump attended.

Robert passed away on October 27, 2013—his 28th birthday. At my request, Mr. Trump eulogized the young man at the funeral Mass. Visibly shaken by this loss, Trump rose to the occasion, his touching words testifying to his character as a man of deep sympathy and generosity.

I crossed Trump's path again three years later at the Alfred Smith Memorial Foundation Dinner at the Waldorf Astoria, the white-tie charitable event hosted annually by the Archbishop of New York. This is where U.S. presidential candidates, mixing good-humored ribbing and fund-raising, share the stage for the last time before the election. In 2016 Trump was no longer just a New York real estate magnate: he was also the Republican Party's choice for president. His rival, the former senator and secretary of state Hillary Clinton, was also in attendance. He told me he remembered my homily at Robert's funeral; I remembered his eulogy. Twenty days later Lou and Robert's faithful friend became the president-elect of the United States.

As I mentioned many pages ago, Pope Benedict, whom I had met at the Council as Father Joseph Ratzinger, resigned his papacy on February 28, 2013. Thirteen days later Cardinal Jorge Mario Bergoglio ascended to the papal throne. During the days of the conclave, I was asked who I thought was eminently *papabile* ("pope-eligible"). I remember New York City's FOX 5 interviewing me on Vatican matters. One day the vice-principal of my parish's school asked me what I thought.

"Don't forget Jorge Bergoglio!" I instantly replied.

"Who?"

"The Archbishop of Buenos Aires."

I was almost alone in predicting this.* On March 13, 2013, he was elected pope and took the name Francis, the first to do so.

Several years earlier I met him briefly during a visit to Argentina to attend the blessing of a school named in honor of my mother, Maria Catalina Scali. She had been the *maestra* (teacher) of many pupils who emigrated from Italy to La Plata, the University City of Buenos Aires. Like me, the archbishop, and now pope was a son of Italian immigrants.

Later that year, on July 1st, I retired from Saint Augustine's. Little did I realize how short my "retirement" would be. Two weeks later I was called to be Advisor to the Permanent Mission of the Holy See to the United Nations; on September 3rd, I was already in my new office at 25 East 39th Street in Manhattan.† There I continue the work of implementing the vision of the popes I've known, and now that means Pope Francis. On that international platform we defend the human rights of the unborn and women (in a world where two-thirds of them are treated like trash), condemn human trafficking, and address the problems of nearly two billion refugees or displaced persons (the collateral damage of wars, about 29 of which now rage

---

* Christie L. Chicoine, "Pastor of Ossining Parish Worked with Future Pope," *Catholic New York*, March 20, 2013, https://cny.org/stories/pastor-of-ossining-parish-worked-with-future-pope,9055.

† The Permanent Mission of the Holy See is different from its state representation in the United States. A nuncio is the pope's ambassador to a country. Where the Vatican doesn't have diplomatic relations, there's an Apostolic Delegation. There was no nuncio to Washington until 1984. When I was stationed in the nation's capital in the late sixties, the Vatican only had an apostolic delegate to handle ecclesiastical matters and relations with the country's bishops and little else.

across the globe). Add to that list famine, the horrific plight of children in conflict areas, and the quest for world peace. Despite difficulties, we contribute to the search for practical, real-world solutions. Our guides are papal exhortations to the United Nations, including those of Paul VI, October 4, 1965[*]; Pope John Paul II, October 2, 1979,[†] and October 5, 1995[‡]; and Pope Benedict, April 18, 2008.[§] This tradition continued with Pope Francis's delivery of the opening address of the General Assembly on September 25, 2015,[¶] and, of course, with his encyclical *Laudato Si'*, already five years old as of this writing.[**]

I've had the privilege of concelebrating Mass with Pope Francis several times in the Santa Marta Chapel (where he says Mass daily), before and after which we had many opportunities to exchange ideas. I gave him some research of mine on the challenges posed by an increase in the median age of the world' population: by 2030, at least 18 percent of the global

---

[*] "Address of the Holy Father Paul VI to the United Nations Organization," October 4, 1965, http://www.vatican.va/content/paul-vi/en/speeches/1965/documents/hf_p-vi_spe_19651004_united-nations.html.

[†] "Address of His Holiness John Paul II to the 34th General Assembly of the United Nations," October 2, 1979, http://www.vatican.va/content/john-paul-ii/en/speeches/1979/october/documents/hf_jp-ii_spe_19791002_general-assembly-onu.html.

[‡] "Address of His Holiness John Paul II, United Nations Headquarters," October 5, 1995, http://www.vatican.va/content/john-paul-ii/en/speeches/1995/october/documents/hf_jp-ii_spe_05101995_address-to-uno.html.

[§] "Address of His Holiness Benedict XVI," April 18, 2008, http://www.vatican.va/content/benedict-xvi/en/speeches/2008/april/documents/hf_ben-xvi_spe_20080418_un-visit.html.

[¶] "Address of the Holy Father," United Nations Headquarters, September 25, 2015, http://www.vatican.va/content/francesco/en/speeches/2015/september/documents/papa-francesco_20150925_onu-visita.html.

[**] "Encyclical Letter *Laudato Si'* of the Holy Father Francis on Care for Our Common Home," May 24, 2015, published June 18, 2015, http://www.vatican.va/content/francesco/en/encyclicals/documents/papa-francesco_20150524_enciclica-laudato-si.html#_ftnref1.

population will be older than 65 years. The problem of welfare of the elderly will loom larger in the coming decades. On September 28, 2014, Pope Francis devoted a special day and Mass in the Vatican for the elderly.

The Permanent Mission of the Holy See hosted Pope Francis when he visited New York to address the United Nations on September 25, 2015.* After a quick early breakfast the next day, he was off to Philadelphia, next on his itinerary. I thought he looked tired and needed to rest, and told him so. Which provoked him to ask me:

"Did you look at yourself in the mirror this morning?"

"No, I didn't have time."

"If you did, you'd see you're the one who looks tired!"

Pope Francis lives out the Church's teaching on the sacrality of life and promotes her efforts on behalf of the world's vulnerable and marginalized. This might make some uncomfortable, but discomfort can be a symptom of growth, of ethical "growing pains." Social controversies, which we will always have with us, often reveal readiness to judge and slowness to understand. Like his predecessors, Pope Francis champions the teachings of the Gospel aimed at leading humanity toward a better world, giving a voice to the unheard and unwelcome without regard to political and financial calculations. While visiting the Varginha community in Rio de Janeiro, Brazil, in 2013, Francis affirmed that:

Everyone, according to their possibilities and responsibilities, should know how to offer their contribution

---

* Pope Francis actually *opened* the General Assembly that year, an honor ordinarily reserved to the President of the Assembly and the Secretary General.

to put an end to so many social injustices. It is not the culture of selfishness, of individualism, which often governs our society, the one that builds and leads to a more habitable world, but the culture of solidarity; see in the other not a competitor or a number, but a brother.*

℮⸨⸨⸩

The statements of the Permanent Mission of the Holy See to the United Nations, which I serve, reflect the Church's social teaching and the pope's teaching magisterium. The Vatican's Permanent Representative to the United Nations, Archbishop Gabriele Caccia, summarized our goals in his intervention at that august body on October 6, 2020:

> During and after the [COVID-19] pandemic, all States should see to it that the elementary conditions needed to ensure dignified and free life exist. This includes protecting and putting into practice the fundamental rights of all persons. At the same time, human rights will never be fully recognized and universally acknowledged unless all States, especially those in conflict, engage in good faith and integrity with this international organization, working together to reach this goal. International consensus requires setting aside ideological conflicts and

---

* "Visit to the Community of Varginha (Manguinhos): Address of Pope Francis," Apostolic Journey to Rio de Janeiro (Brazil) on the occasion of the 28th World Youth Day, July 25, 2013, http://www.vatican.va/content/francesco/en/speeches/2013/july/documents/papa-francesco_20130725_gmg-comunita-varginha.html.

also conceptions of the human person in which the dignity, rights and freedoms of the other are not respected.[*]

We must be concrete when we speak about such things. On July 16, 2015, heads of state met in Addis Ababa, Ethiopia, on the Sustainable Development Fund. This level meeting was called AAAA, for "Addis Ababa Action Agenda." A week later, on July 25th, the UN General Assembly approved the meeting's decisions. When it was presented again a year later at the UN, however, nothing had been implemented! I pointed out that the word "action" in the meeting's title means *action*, just as "agenda" is Latin for "things to be *done*"!

In a nutshell, what I do at the UN continues the work I did in the Vatican for 26 years: assisting the Holy Father in his multifaceted work as Supreme Pontiff of the Catholic Church and sovereign of the Vatican City-State. (All dicasteries of the Roman Curia do this, of course, each in its own way.) As busy as this work might keep me, I'm free to offer my services, sacramental and pastoral, to the parish of Our Savior in Manhattan. Even when assisting Bishop Sheen, if I were free on a Sunday, I'd say Mass at Saint Clare's in the Bronx or, when in Washington, at Saint Jude's in Rockville, Maryland. When in Rome, I'd celebrate Mass in any number of churches in the Eternal City or outside its walls. Wherever I was assigned, I'd try to find a parish where I could help out, simply because the exercise of my priesthood has been, is, and I hope will be

---

[*] "Vatican Tells UN It Is 'Deeply Concerned' by Push to 'Reinterpret' Foundations of Human Rights," Catholic News Agency, October 7, 2020, https://www.catholic newsagency.com/news/vatican-tells-un-it-is-deeply-concerned-by-pressure-to -reinterpret-the-very-foundations-of-human-rights-95796.

until the end, the quintessential element of this "kid from the Bronx."

But that kid never forgot the teachings and inspiration of his father, who insisted that I "take care of the people," especially people in need. And so, dear reader, I'd be remiss if I closed out this chapter without emphasizing that serving the interests of the less fortunate has never taken second place to anything else in my long life, with the exception, just noted, of the priesthood. I'm keenly aware that when I face the Eternal Judge (Matthew 25:21), He's not going to care about what I've accumulated materially. He's going to evaluate my life according to how consistently I've recognized and served Him in the poor, the hungry, the thirsty, the naked, the strangers, the sick, and the imprisoned.

I was the "angel" who erased Bishop Sheen's blackboard as he delivered a talk on *Life Is Worth Living* in 1967 during which he brought to the world's attention, as only he could, the significance of the 30th parallel.* As he ran his green marker on a map along that parallel, he described it as a fateful line of demarcation: above it live the people who control over 90 percent of the world's wealth, the remaining 10 percent being distributed among those below it. I've tried to contribute to the narrowing of that scandalous divide by encouraging sentiments of generosity in those whose material riches afford them opportunities to make a difference in the lives of millions, even billions, of people.

With that motivation, I organized a presentation to Pope Francis by members of the Fortune-Time Global Forum, chief

---

* You can view "Fulton Sheen: The 30th Parallel" on YouTube: https://www.youtube.com/watch?v=GdAkTeQVKR8.

executive officers all, which met in the Vatican on December 2–3, 2016. During an audience granted by the Holy Father, he encouraged them to share their insights as well as their wealth:

> I encourage you to continue the work you have begun at this Forum and to seek ever more creative ways to transform our institutions and economic structures so that they may be able to respond to the needs of our day and be in service of the human person, especially those marginalized and discarded.*

Three months later, however, nothing concrete had resulted. I expressed my disappointment to a lady who had been in the audience, Lady Lynn Forester de Rothschild. Her good cheer was infectious, and so together we brainstormed a follow-up to the forum, namely, a "Council for Inclusive Capitalism." This would build on the willingness of some of those CEOs to take seriously the pope's exhortation.

One hundred eighty-one CEOs proposed something like this council at a business roundtable on August 19, 2019. They entertained the idea that corporations should replace their traditional exclusive goal of maximizing shareholder profits with a commitment to balancing the interests of shareholders with those of stakeholders, that is, customers, employees, suppliers, and local communities.

I was with the Board of the Council for Inclusive Capitalism when, on November 11, 2019, Pope Francis received a select

---

* "Greeting of His Holiness Pope Francis to Participants of the Fortune-Time Global Forum," December 3, 2016, http://www.vatican.va/content/francesco/en/speeches/2016/december/documents/papa-francesco_20161203_imprenditori.html.

group of CEOs committed to enacting this proposal. Pope Francis told us:

> During my meeting three years ago with participants in the Fortune-Time Global Forum 2016, I addressed the need for more inclusive and equitable economic models that would permit each person to share in the resources of this world and have opportunities to realize his or her potential. The 2016 Forum allowed for an exchange of ideas and information aimed at creating a more humane economy and contributing to the eradication of poverty on the global level. Your Council is one of the results of the 2016 Forum. You have taken up the challenge of realizing the vision of the Forum by seeking ways to make capitalism become a more inclusive instrument for integral human well-being.[*]

"Actions speak louder than words!" Saint Anthony of Padua (1195-1231) aphorized for the ages. "Let your words teach and your actions speak!" It is my fervent prayer, and my earthly life's last desire, that something great, historically meaningful, *and most of all concrete* will emerge from these efforts to eradicate global poverty.

---

[*] "Address of His Holiness Pope Francis to the Members of the Council for Inclusive Capitalism," November 11, 2019, http://www.vatican.va/content/francesco/en/speeches/2019/november/documents/papa-francesco_20191111_consiglio-capitalismo-inclusivo.html.

TWELVE

The Church of Benedict, Francis, and the Future

The unity of the Church is always in danger, for centuries.
It has been throughout its entire history.
Wars, internal conflicts, centrifugal pushes,
threats of schism. But in the end, the consciousness
that the Church is and must remain
united has always prevailed.

POPE EMERITUS BENEDICT XVI*

---

* From an interview in *Corriere della Sera*, June 28, 2019, https://www.corriere.it/
sette/incontri/19_giugno_28/uomo-che-veglia-vaticano-7-dialogo-benedetto
-xvi-bdd399a4-98d4-11e9-a7fc-0829f3644f7a.shtml, as translated from the
Italian in Gerard O'Connell, "Pope Benedict XVI Speaks in New Interview:
'There Is One Pope, He Is Francis,'" *America: The Jesuit Review*, June 28, 2019, https://
www.americamagazine.org/faith/2019/06/28/pope-benedict-xvi-speaks-new
-interview-there-one-pope-he-francis.

I cannot conclude without mentioning what I lived through and saw regarding events that affected the Church's reputation, which has been tarnished by numerous headline-making events.

The clerical sexual abuse scandal, which has harmed the Church's reputation, has a number of possible causes. One is moral relativism. In 2010, Pope Benedict XVI published an essay in which he offered a unified perspective on the sexual abuse scandal. One main reason, he wrote, was the effort by several prominent theologians for a relativistic perspective on morality where "there could no longer be anything that constituted an absolute good, any more than anything fundamentally evil; [there could be] only relative value judgments."*

There were also faulty psychological theories that held that pedophile priests need only a change of venue and could, with

---

* Pope Benedict XVI, "The Church and the Scandal of Sexual Abuse," Catholic News Agency, April 12, 2019, https://www.catholicnewsagency.com/news/full-text-of-benedict-xvi-the-church-and-the-scandal-of-sexual-abuse-59639.

counseling, be rehabilitated. This view, widely promulgated in the 1970s, turned out to be catastrophic for the Church.

When I worked at the Congregation for the Clergy, we had the responsibility to handle such problems as they were brought to us and to suggest solutions. I remember the first such case I had to handle. That was in 1986, and it concerned an abusive priest from a small diocese in Texas. That diocese's bishop followed our directives, and things went smoothly. When we shared our way of treating such cases with others in the American hierarchy, they told us not to worry. According to them, pedophile priests would be a transient phenomenon.

I remember informing the bishops of a study that concluded that pedophilia is an incurable disease. One might imply that it is curable when one moves the patient from parish to parish, or from facility to facility. That is not so. It is now common knowledge that both popes, Benedict and Francis, have strongly, consistently, and repeatedly condemned child abuse by priests and taken severe action against the offenders. More significantly, the Church has set up reporting systems and initiated speedy and full investigations when allegations against the clergy are made. Consequently, such abuses now occur infrequently, although even one case is one too many.

I often have to remind people that the Church is not just the pope, his brother bishops, and priests. It's also the laity. Since we've all fallen short of God's standards, all of us who are Catholic have our part to play in conforming the Church to the image of Christ.

On April 6, 1964, the Vatican was granted Permanent Observer status at the United Nations, which was founded in 1945 in San Francisco. Two years later, in 1947, when I was still a teenager, the UN's future headquarters in New York City began to rise on the banks of the East River in the neighborhood of Turtle Bay. The emergence of this huge box impressed me. At the time, of course, I had no idea what this international body was going to do, the mission it would have, or the role it would play in history, let alone my little part in that history.

But three-quarters of a century later, it's clear to me that although the UN has accomplished some good things, we could have done much more through it. Despite our economic strength, we're not doing enough.

Something's missing. Global indifference, I suggest, is the culprit.

Ours.

The Lord asked Cain, "Where's your brother?"

"I'm not my brother's keeper" was the murderer's reply.

In 1994, to give one example, 800,000 people were killed in Rwanda in a hundred days. How did we let that happen? Could we not have done *something* to avert that atrocity? That sin is our legacy. Future generations will not judge kindly our indifference, which borders on complicity.

When the UN was born, it was greeted with much enthusiasm. My ministry began in the optimistic fifties. The Second World War was in our rearview mirror. There was much to rebuild in Europe, and the Marshall Plan helped rebuild it. The task was enormous, but we rolled up our sleeves and got to work. Europeans knew where we stood: Herr Schicklgruber, that Berlin fiend, was not going to have the last word. There was little global indifference then; today it finds fertile soil in our smugness. "I'm all right. Who else matters?" Coming out of that war we embodied almost a familial attitude that cried, "Hey, let's get this done!"

On February 28, 2013, Pope Benedict XVI announced, in an emotional but polished Latin speech, his resignation from the papacy. This shocked not only the world, but also most members of the Roma Curia.

It did not come as a complete surprise to me. I had long been convinced that Benedict had accepted the burden of the papacy only out of obedience to God's will.

The recent movie *The Two Popes* gives the impression that it was Ratzinger who pursued the papacy, while Bergoglio was almost indifferent to the prospect of occupying Peter's throne. The truth is almost the exact opposite. Unfortunately, many people will come away from this exercise in disinformation, confident that they know what happened. After all, they saw the movie!

I know that Cardinal Ratzinger, who had suffered a hemorrhagic stroke in 1991, once asked John Paul II to allow him to retire. He wanted to return to Marktl, his hometown in Germany, to live out the rest of his life with his brother, Georg, a life dedicated to prayer, studying, writing, and preparing for the Lord's eventual call. The pope refused this request. The rest is history. I was present when, on April 8, 2005, as Dean of the

College of Cardinals, Ratzinger gave a homily at John Paul II's funeral. It was a detailed program for a future pope to follow. Little did he know that he would be that pontiff.

During the conclave that elected Ratzinger, Jorge Bergoglio was one of the most prominent of the *papabili* (candidates for the papacy). Contrary to the impression conveyed by the aforementioned movie, had Bergoglio been chosen in 2005, he would have at once exclaimed "*Accepto!*"

I had the privilege of requesting papal audiences for Rabbi Arthur Schneier, senior rabbi of Park East Synagogue in New York City, with Pope Benedict XVI* and Pope Francis, who made him a Papal Knight.† Cardinal Timothy Dolan conferred this knighthood on April 27, 2015, at the residence of the Permanent Mission of the Holy See to the United Nations.‡

Rabbi Schneier had also requested audience with Pope Francis for 30 members of the United Jewish Appeal Federation, and this was granted on November 6, 2013. Attending to the guests, I took former Secretary of State

---

* "Rabbi Arthur Schneier Meets with Pope Benedict XVI to Discuss the Urgent Need to Protect Religious Sites Around the World," Appeal of Conscience Foundation (Rome), May 2001, https://appealofconscience.org/timeline/rome -italy-rabbi-arthur-schneier-meets-with-pope-benedict-xvi-to-discuss-the-urgent -need-to-protect-religious-sites-around-the-world/.

† "Pope Francis Names Rabbi Arthur Schneier Papal Knight," Appeal of Conscience Foundation (Rome), April 27, 2015. https://appealofconscience.org/ pope-francis-names-rabbi-arthur-schneier-papal-knight/.

‡ James Barron, "Cardinal Timothy Dolan Confers a Rare Papal Knighthood on Rabbi Arthur Schneier," *New York Times*, April 28, 2015, https://www.nytimes .com/2015/04/28/nyregion/cardinal-timothy-dolan-confers-a-rare-papal- knighthood-on-rabbi-arthur-schneier.html.

Henry Kissinger to the reception area on the second floor. We had to take an ancient elevator, whose cab looked like a relic of the Industrial Revolution. After we squeezed in (barely), I shut the cab's metallic gate. It crawled excruciatingly slowly, almost imperceptibly so. But we had no choice: the eminent nonagenarian could not climb stairs.

"Monsignor, are you sure we'll get to the second floor?"

I reassured him that we would, and we did.

As the end of my ninth decade approaches, I'm equally amazed that I can transfer so much of the inner sanctum of my mind to the external hard drive of this book.

Not long ago, though, I realized I couldn't take these conditions for granted. How much longer could I ignore either the facts of aging or the importuning of friends? Precious recollections could at any moment be buried or sandblasted away by accident, and there'd be no second chance. I therefore undertook to record as much as I could of what I witnessed during my priestly life across nearly seven decades, focusing on encounters with popes, canonized saints among them, as well as saints who weren't popes. I hope cameos of some of the nonclerical *dramatis personae* who also walked onto my life's stage have enriched your reading experience.

As a power of the human spirit, memory is as great as it is mysterious. When we record our memories, we contribute to a history that, as Cicero aphorized, is the teacher of life; when we exercise this power, we preserve it.* Use it or lose it. I hope I've used it well.

There's more sand at the bottom of my hourglass than the top, but I'm buoyed up by the prospect of Everlasting Life with Christ and my many family members and friends who have gone to the Lord's home ahead of me. With the assistance and friendship of many, spiritual giants among them (a grace I never expected), I've tried to serve Jesus as a priest during some of the Church's most exciting, challenging, even tumultuous times under six popes. As God's steward and witness, I share these remembrances to remind you that He loves you and will never abandon you.

There are many other stories (episodes) in my life that could have been written in this book, but I have refrained from writing them, either because I feel that they would not be of interest to my gracious reader (lector) or because it is better that they may not be told.

---

* *Historia magistra vitae* ("History is the teacher of life") is from *De Oratore* ("On the Orator"); *Memoria minuitur nisi eam exerceas* ("Your power of memory will diminish unless you exercise it"), from *De Senectute, De Amicitia, De Divinatione* ("On Old Age. On Friendship. On Divination").

Acknowledgments

For many years, friends and others have urged me to write this book. Until now, however, I've always withstood their gentle pressure, either because my duties made it easy to decline, or simply because I was hesitant to divulge matters that belong in the archives in the bin marked "ancient history."

But then one day a great friend virtually cornered me into committing this act of recollection. You owe this book to Christopher Ruddy, media entrepreneur and man of great faith. He set everything in motion, helping me push past lingering apprehensions and putting resources at my disposal. Among them was Anthony Flood, who over the course of a year met and corresponded with me, recorded my recollections, and smoothed their transcriptions into the narrative you're now holding. Mary Glenn, publisher of Humanix Books, also has my gratitude for her expert and patient orchestration of the production process.

And, let me thank *in absentia* all those personages who have crowded these pages, important personalities as well as my earthly family and the common people by whose wisdom I have been illumined and whose example has guided my existence. To them, and, most of all, to God Almighty and to His Blessed Mother, my humble and profound gratitude!

Index

About the Author

Monsignor Hilary C. Franco is Advisor at the Permanent Observer of the Holy See to the United Nations. An active member of the Catholic Biblical Association of America, he has been the recipient of several international awards, including Solemare 1988 in Taormina, Italy, for the popular international television programs *Life Is Worth Living* and *The Bishop Sheen Show*. He also received at the Teatro "La Scala" in Milano, Italy, the first Civiltà Senza Frontiere award, which was conferred also on that occasion to the Nobel Peace Prize Laureate Mother Teresa of Calcutta and to 1986 Nobel Prize for Medicine Laureate Professor Rita Levi Montalcini.

Monsignor Franco is a Knight of the Equestrian Order of the Holy Sepulchre of Jerusalem, which bestowed on him a Cross for his service of 20 years as Representative of the Eastern Lieutenancy of the United States at the headquarters of the order in Rome. He is a Magisterial Chaplain of the Sovereign Military Hospitaller Order of Saint John of Jerusalem, of Rhodes and of Malta.

Monsignor Franco was educated in the United States and Italy. He was ordained a priest as an alumnus of the Pontifical Roman Seminary at the rather young age of 22 years. He received a doctorate in biblical theology from the Pontifical Lateran University in Rome, graduating *magna cum laude*, when he was not yet 24. He earned a master's degree in sociology from Fordham University in New York and later received a degree in canon law (JCL) at the Lateran University.

In the summer of 1956, he served as Assistant Pastor at the Church of Our Lady of Mount Carmel, in the Bronx, and then served as Assistant Pastor at Saint Dominic's Church, also in the Bronx, and at the Assumption Parish in Staten Island. Beginning in 1962, he was Assistant to Bishop Fulton J. Sheen, at the National Office of the Propagation of the Faith in New York. While in that office, he was a member of the Board of Editors of *World Mission* magazine, and also contributed biblical articles to the *New Catholic Encyclopedia*. He also worked on the preparation of conciliar documents for the Second Vatican Council, which he attended as a *peritus* (expert) for the American Council Fathers.

In 1967, after a few months' assignment at Our Lady of Victory Parish in Mount Vernon, New York, he was called to serve in the Diplomatic Corps of the Vatican at the Apostolic Delegation in Washington, DC (a "first" for a New York priest). The following year he was named an Official of the Prefecture for Economic Affairs of the Holy See at the Vatican. He remained there for 2 years, until he was named Official of the Congregation for the Clergy at the Vatican, where he served for 24 years as the person in charge of the "English Desk," which he had initiated.

He was named a Monsignor in 1971 and a Prelate of His Holiness in 1981. He has been Pastor of Saint Augustine's Church in Ossining for 19 years, since September 1994, and he has also been a Judge of the Interdiocesan (for the whole state of New York) Ecclesiastical Tribunal (the Court of Appeals for the Province of New York). He is also currently a member of the Advisory Board for the Cause of Beatification of Archbishop Fulton J. Sheen and a board member of the Pontifical Path to Peace Foundation. He has been a frequent television commentator discussing Vatican and Church topics on Fox, NBC, Newsmax, and RAI (the main Italian television network).